Agile Methodologies In-Depth

Delivering Proven Agile, SCRUM and Kanban
Practices for High-Quality Business Demands

Sudipta Malakar

www.bpbonline.com

FIRST EDITION 2021

Copyright © BPB Publications, India

ISBN: 978-93-89328-561

Distributors:

BPB PUBLICATIONS
20, Ansari Road, Darya Ganj
New Delhi-110002
Ph: 23254990/23254991

DECCAN AGENCIES
4-3-329, Bank Street,
Hyderabad-500195
Ph: 24756967/24756400

MICRO MEDIA
Shop No. 5, Mahendra Chambers,
150 DN Rd. Next to Capital Cinema,
V.T. (C.S.T.) Station, MUMBAI-400 001
Ph: 22078296/22078297

BPB BOOK CENTRE
376 Old Lajpat Rai Market,
Delhi-110006
Ph: 23861747

To View Complete
BPB Publications Catalogue
Scan the QR Code:

Published by Manish Jain for BPB Publications, 20 Ansari Road, Darya Ganj, New Delhi-110002 and Printed by him at Repro India Ltd, Mumbai

www.bpbonline.com

Dedicated to

My wife Sangita and my son Shreyan

About the Author

Sudipta Malakar is an accomplished SAP practice area head, Certified IT Sr. program manager, Agile coach – Advanced level,, Harvard Business School, USA, alumnus, patent holder, and an International bestselling author & speaker with more than 17 years of experience in directing SAP DEV teams in supporting many major Global fortune 500 clients in multiple large accounts.

He is a certified sr. program manager (MSP practitioner), a sr. project manager (PRINCE2 Practitioner), PMP®, CSP®, ITIL(F), a certified Agile Leader(CDL), CLMM, CMM, and an advanced certified Scrum Master (A-CSM) ®, CSPO®, CSM®, KMP2, KMP1, ICP-ACC®, TKP®, ISO 9001 Lead Auditor, Lean Six Sigma Master Black Belt, CMMi (Expert).

He worked in various IT companies like IBM, Wipro, Satyam, Tech Mahindra, Patni, and Syntel, and he played a crucial sr. management/Agile coach role for various global clients like Sterlite, Lufthansa, Nestle, PMI, Suncor, IPA, Canadian Pacific railways, Sony, Volvo, Allstate, and BOC Linde.

LinkedIn: **https://www.linkedin.com/in/sudipta-malakar-csp-klmm-cdl-kmm-cspo-kmp-a-csm-icp-acc-tkp-3a794213a/**

About the Reviewer

Aditya has industry experience of 12 years, and he has lead many Agile transformations. He has worked on multiple Agile frameworks. Aditya is currently a SAFe Certified practitioner (SPC) working on aSAFe implementation in FireEye. During his career in Tesco and Sophos, he has worked on Scrum. He was instrumental in the rollout of Scrum in Sophos, where he helped other Scrum Masters with Agile and Scrum's concepts. He has conducted many Agile trainings and talks in his organization. Many of the Scrum Master and Product Owners have rated his trainings very highly. In his current organization, he was the first Scrum Master in India, and he had led the teams from Scrum and SAFe transformation journey. He believes in making the world a better place through Agile, and books help spread knowledge faster.

Acknowledgement

No task is a single man's effort. Cooperation and coordination of various people at different levels go into successful implementation of this book. At the outset, I am thankful to the almighty constantly and invisibly guiding everybody for helping me work on the right path.

My father, Shri Ganesh Chandra Malakar, is a retired professor, and I am indebted to him for his support in reaching this milestone. My loving mother, Smt. Sikha Malakar, always inspires me, and my loving son, Shreyan Malakar, my elder brother Shri Sabyasachi Malakar and my wife, Smt. Sangita Malakar, are always supporting me at their level best.

I am thankful to my parents, spouse, son, family, and my mentors (Mr. Todd Little, Chairman of Kanban University, USA, Mr. Julian Birkinshaw, Dean & Professor of London Business School, Mr. Clayton M. Christensen, Professor of Harvard Business School - USA and Father of Global Innovations, disruption, & growth strategy, Mr. David J Anderson - Creator of Kanban Method and CEO, David J Anderson School of Management, J.J. Sutherland - CEO of Scrum, Inc., Dave Litten – CEO of Projex Academy, Mike Cohn - CST, Nanda Lankalapalli - CST, Peter Stevens - CST, Abid Quereshi - CST, Brian Tracy - CEO of Brian Tracy International) for their guidance that motivated me to work for the betterment of consultants by writing this book with sincerity and honesty. This book wouldn't have been possible without their support.

I would also like to thank the publisher and the whole staff at BPB Publications, especially Mr. Manish Jain for their motivation and for making this text presentable.

Finally, I would like to thank everyone who has directly or indirectly contributed to complete this authentic work.

Preface

This book is for businesses that aspire to improve business agility, deliver fit-for-purpose products and services, delight customers, and provide the security of long-term survival associated with mature businesses that consistently meet or exceed customer expectations. Learn a lean approach by seeing how Kanban made a difference in four real-world situations. You'll explore how different teams used Kanban to make paradigm-changing improvements in software development. These teams were struggling with overwork, unclear priorities, and lack of direction. As you discover what worked for them, you'll understand how to make significant changes in real-life situations. Change is difficult, but the US government is also going agile. Are you aware that *"The brain processes visual information 60,000 times faster than text?"*

The Artefact has been developed as a resource to understand, evaluate, and use agile and hybrid agile approaches. This practice guide provides guidance on when, where, and how to apply agile approaches and provides practical tools for practitioners and organizations to increase agility. It will also help you in PMI-ACP and SAFe Exam preparation.

If you are a student, parent, graduate hire, tech developer, IT consultant, agile coach, scrum master, product owner, leader, manager, corporate change agent, CXOs, senior manager, part of a product management team, or an IT operator/OPS, this book is perfect for you to increase profitability, exceed productivity goals, and elevate work culture through Agile KANBAN, XP, FDD, DSDM, SCRUMBAN, and SCRUM methodology.

This book is single source, comprehensive action guide for business and IT leaders, explains how to increase IT delivery capabilities through the use of Agile and Kanban. Factoring in constant change, communication, a sense of urgency, clear and measurable goals, political realities, and infrastructure needs, it covers all the ingredients required for success. To make things easier for busy students, parents, IT leaders and executives, this book is an indispensable artefact.

This book promises to be a very good starting point for beginners and an asset for those with an insight toward agility. It also articulates how Agile is mapped to traditional practices along with critical success factors of adopting business agility.

Solving a client's issue may require many complex work streams, so we set up a sprint...It's a way of getting people to be collaborative, take accountability and feel empowered.

- TAMARA INGRAM
Chief Executive Officer,
J. Walter Thompson Company

It is said *"To err is human, to forgive divine"*. Although the book is written with sincerity and honesty, I wish that the shortcomings of the book will be forgiven in this light. I am also open to constructive criticism and any suggestions for further improvement. All intelligent suggestions are welcome, and I will try my best to incorporate the invaluable suggestions in the subsequent editions of this book.

Downloading the coloured images:

Please follow the link to download the
Coloured Images of the book:

https://rebrand.ly/2c4ab

Errata

We take immense pride in our work at BPB Publications and follow best practices to ensure the accuracy of our content to provide with an indulging reading experience to our subscribers. Our readers are our mirrors, and we use their inputs to reflect and improve upon human errors, if any, that may have occurred during the publishing processes involved. To let us maintain the quality and help us reach out to any readers who might be having difficulties due to any unforeseen errors, please write to us at :

errata@bpbonline.com

Your support, suggestions and feedbacks are highly appreciated by the BPB Publications' Family.

Did you know that BPB offers eBook versions of every book published, with PDF and ePub files available? You can upgrade to the eBook version at www.bpbonline.com and as a print book customer, you are entitled to a discount on the eBook copy. Get in touch with us at :

business@bpbonline.com for more details.

At **www.bpbonline.com**, you can also read a collection of free technical articles, sign up for a range of free newsletters, and receive exclusive discounts and offers on BPB books and eBooks.

BPB is searching for authors like you

If you're interested in becoming an author for BPB, please visit **www.bpbonline.com** and apply today. We have worked with thousands of developers and tech professionals, just like you, to help them share their insight with the global tech community. You can make a general application, apply for a specific hot topic that we are recruiting an author for, or submit your own idea.

The code bundle for the book is also hosted on GitHub at **https://github.com/bpbpublications/Agile-Methodologies-In-depth**. In case there's an update to the code, it will be updated on the existing GitHub repository.

We also have other code bundles from our rich catalog of books and videos available at **https://github.com/bpbpublications**. Check them out!

PIRACY

If you come across any illegal copies of our works in any form on the internet, we would be grateful if you would provide us with the location address or website name. Please contact us at **business@bpbonline.com** with a link to the material.

If you are interested in becoming an author

If there is a topic that you have expertise in, and you are interested in either writing or contributing to a book, please visit **www.bpbonline.com**.

REVIEWS

Please leave a review. Once you have read and used this book, why not leave a review on the site that you purchased it from? Potential readers can then see and use your unbiased opinion to make purchase decisions, we at BPB can understand what you think about our products, and our authors can see your feedback on their book. Thank you!

For more information about BPB, please visit **www.bpbonline.com**.

Table of Contents

Introduction

Change is difficult, and changing culture is even more difficult. Adopting Agile, Scrum, XP, and KANBAN requires a change of culture and mindset. Many organizations and teams have made many Agile, KANBAN, and Scrum implementation mistakes during the transition. As you discover what worked for them, you'll understand how to make significant changes in real situations. Change is difficult, but the US government is also going agile. Are you aware that *"The brain processes visual information 60,000 times faster than text?"*

Your team is stressed, and the priorities are unclear. Too much work and too little time? You're not sure what your teammates are working on, and management isn't helping. You/your team are encountering overreaching, causing an aborted start, false summit plateaus, and failure to realize full benefit. The attrition rate is too high. If your team is struggling with any of these things, these four case studies will guide you to project success. You can see how Kanban was used to significantly improve time to market and to create a shared focus across marketing, IT, and operations. It will also help you in PMI-ACP and SAFe Exam preparation.

You / your team is planning for enterprise Agile adoption, but you are not aware of Agile SCRUM Kanban Metrics, roadmap, and concrete actions, which enable organizations to achieve fitness-for-purpose and exceptional business agility.

You/your team is planning to use Scrum to develop innovative products and services that delight your customers, increase employee satisfaction, win in the marketplace, enhance customer/business delight and capture new business. But you are not aware of Agile Scrum XP best practices, pitfalls and anti-patterns.

You are students or parents lost in your hectic daily schedules, due to which you missed your milestones. You lost your health in anxiety and overthinking. Tomorrow is your job interview or Agile written assessment(s), but you are anxious over how to pass it with flying colors.

"Agile Adoption Mistakes You Must Avoid" is for people familiar with Agile, KANBAN and Scrum and have a basic knowledge of Agile and Scrum. To learn about the basics of Scrum, read the free downloadable KANBAN artefact by *David J. Anderson & Scrum Guide*, the official Scrum body of knowledge, by *Ken SCWHABER* and *Jeff Sutherland*.

The examples given in this book are user-focused and have been updated with topics, figures, and examples. The book features real-life approaches with examples covering topics from simple to complex and addressing several core concepts and advance topics.

The book is divided into the following sections:

- Pitfalls of the Traditional Waterfall model and the key success factors for adopting Agile SCRUM Kanban in any organization/projects/programs and field rules for faster performance & better results

- Use of Agile for students and parents

- Portfolio/ Upstream Kanban implementations lessons learnt and key takeaways

- PMI-ACP and SAFe exam preparation

- Interview questions and answers on Agile SCRUM, XP, DSDM, KANBAN and SCRUMBAN

- Agile & Kanban Metrics

- JIRA tool use in projects/programs

- Hybrid Agile, Agile SHIFT Framework, and different types of Agile contracts

- How Agile is mapped to traditional practices, along with critical success factors of adopting business agility

- Lessons learnt and pragmatic approach – Agile Scrum Kanban

- Common Agile SCRUM KANBAN misconceptions

- Key takeaways

- Glossary

- Quiz session

CHAPTER 1

Key Success Factors for Adopting Agile SCRUM Kanban in Any Organizations

Introduction

Agile began as an iterative, collaborative, value-driven approach to developing software. It was originally conceived as a framework to help structure work on complex projects with dynamic, unpredictable characteristics. But since then, it has evolved into somewhat of a philosophy or world view with a set of well-articulated values and principles that it shares with Agile's many varieties.

Let's discuss some of the top benefits of organizational agility.

Figure 1.1: *The top benefits of organizational agility (Image Source: leankanban.com)*

Based on our research findings and conversations with top executives, we discovered that Agile methodologies can help spur growth and support digital transformation in an era of high customer demand and fast-emerging market trends. The report shows Agile organizations experience:

- Faster time to market (60%)
- Faster innovation (59%)
- Improved non-financial results such as customer experience and product quality (59%)
- Improved employee morale (57%)

The essence of Agile development:

- Lean – eliminate waste
- Iterative – embrace change
- Incremental delivery – promote feedback
- Value-driven – enhanced ROI, reduced risk
- Collaborative – customer involvement
- Quality-focused – potentially shippable product
- Bring a just-in-time product management perspective to IT projects

An Agile Team!

The Agile team is a co-located, cross-functional, self-directed group of individuals who are self-sufficient as a team and have the ability and authority to perform to deliver business values in short iteration time box.

What is Agile?

Let's see what Agile is.

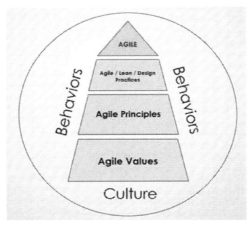

Figure 1.2: *What is Agile (Image source: https://www.scrumalliance.org)*

What is Scrum?

Scrum is a simple yet incredibly powerful set of principles and practices that help teams deliver products in short cycles, enabling fast feedback, continual improvement, and rapid adaptation to change.

Scrum refers to a holistic or *"rugby"* approach—where teams go the distance as a unit, passing the ball back and forth—as opposed to the traditional sequential or "relay race" approach for managing new product development.

What is SCRUM

Let's see what Scrum is.

Figure 1.3: What is SCRUM (Image source: https://www.scrumalliance.org)

BEIJING Olympics - Men's relay anchor Tyson Gay, part of the American team that won the relay at last year's World Championships, dropped the baton from third-leg runner *Darvish Patton.*

Structure

In this chapter, we will discuss the following topics:

- Agile manifesto
- Agile principles
- Key agile principles
- Agile values
- Traditional life cycle versus agile development
- Agile mapped to traditional practices
- Agility versus agile
- The state of agility

- Three steps to increase agility
- Agile framework
- Agile concepts
- Benefits of agile
- Agile contracts nuts and bolts
- Backlog management in agile
- Agile contracts - modeling a transformation in contracting
- Role of manager (people) in an agile organization
- Agile estimation and planning at program and portfolio level
- Agile budget management
- Managing bottlenecks with KANBAN
- What is KANBAN
- Kanban general practices
- Why KANBAN
- Benefits of KANBAN
- 10 things about KANBAN
- Six forms of proto KANBAN
- Sample KANBAN board
- KANBAN card template
- KANBAN and incident categorization - example
- Jira ticket/user profile
- Jira tool best practice – dashboard
- KANBAN - critical & emergency events
- 5 enabling agile ways of working across the organization
- The agile shift framework
- The new role of the manager
- KANBAN vs. scrum

Objectives

After studying this unit, you should be able to:

- Understand the concept(s) of Agile, Scrum, and Kanban
- Apply Agile, Scrum, and Kanban in your organization/project(s)
- Understand the pitfalls of the traditional waterfall model
- Understand the field rules for faster performance and better results

- Understand the critical success factors of adopting Agile over the Waterfall model

1.1 Agile Manifesto

Agile Manifesto, 2001 Snowbird, Utah, is a statement of 4 values and 12 principles that summarize the thinking of the agile perspective and methodologies. Even though agile methods predated the manifesto by several years, it is considered the founding document of agile.

What is Agile Manifesto?

The agile manifesto was created during a meeting in February 2001 that brought together a number of software and methodology experts who were in the forefront of the emerging agile methods. The people in attendance are shown in the following image:

Figure 1.4: Agile Manifesto, 2001 Snowbird, Utah (Image Source: http://agilemanifesto.org/)

The Agile Alliance provides some background on the genesis of Agile methods:

In the late 1990s, several methodologies began to gain public attention. Each had a different combination of old ideas, new ideas, and transmuted old ideas, but they all emphasized close collaboration between the programmer team and business experts; face-to-face communication (as more efficient than written documentation); frequent delivery of new deployable business value; tight, self-organizing teams; and ways to craft the code and the team such that the inevitable requirements churn was not a crisis [Agile Alliance 2001c].

A group of software industry practitioners and consultants, who came to be known as the Agile Alliance, developed and published key tenets known as the Agile Manifesto for Software Development [Agile Alliance 2001]:

Agile Manifesto

We are uncovering better ways of developing software by doing it and helping others do it.
Through this work we have come to value:

Individuals and interactions over processes and tools
Working software over comprehensive documentation
Customer collaboration over contract negotiation
Responding to change over following a plan

While there is value in the items on the right, we value the items on the left more.

Figure 1.5: Agile Manifesto (Image Source: AgileAlliance.org)

The four values of the Agile Manifesto are written in the format "A over B" to address intention, focus, and effort.

Illustration of Agile Manifesto

The four values of the Agile Manifesto aren't saying *"Do A instead of B"*. Instead, they acknowledge that both A and B will be components of our projects but say that we should apply more of our focus, emphasis, and intention to A than to B:

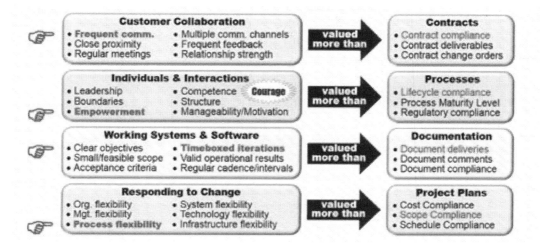

Figure 1.6: Agile Manifesto illustration (Image Source: AgileAlliance.org)

It is important to note that none of the elements on the right-hand side of the list are absent; rather, they support and add value to the elements on the left-hand side of the list:

- Tools and processes facilitate interactions between team members, as opposed to shoehorning these interactions into molds and patterns for the sake of process compliance.

- Documentation is developed to add value to development and sustenance of the code rather than as evidence to prove compliance or completion.

Contract negotiations must establish a collaborative work environment that enables effective decision making and flexible response, rather than high overhead change control processes. (This can also include early termination points to limit government risk for poor performance.)

High-level plans must be flexible to allow for the necessary evolution of system requirements; plans become more granular at the development level.

1.2 Agile Principles

In addition to the four agile values, the authors of the Manifesto created twelve guiding principles for agile methods. This part of the Manifesto reads as follows:

- Begin with clarity about WHY, HOW, and WHAT over WHAT, HOW, and WHY. Start with outcome, not output, and follow it all across the journey.

- Inspect, adapt, improve, and sustain the business outcome.
- Encourage self-direction for teams to uncover innovation, instead of concentrating leadership in the hands of a select few.

In other words:
- Focus on customer and business value
- Iterative and fast
- Flexible, adaptive, and continuously improving
- Collaboration and teamwork
- Empowered and self-directed teams

Let's take a closer look at each of the Agile Manifestos twelve principles. Again, although the principles may use software development terms, as you read about them, think about how these concepts apply to other types of knowledge work projects.

Interpretation of Agile Principles

- Highest priority is customer satisfaction, achieved by the early and consistent delivery of valuable software OR *"Satisfy customer with great systems"*.
- Welcome the changing requirements, even those that arise late in development OR *"Welcome change"*.
- Continuous focus on delivering shippable customer priority deliverables in an iterative and incremental way. Working software is frequently delivered, from a couple of weeks or months; shorter timescale is more preferred to use OR *"Deliver frequently"*.
- The business folk and developers must work together throughout the project OR *"Work with business"*.
- Projects are built around motivated individuals - support and trust them to successfully accomplish the job OR *"Motivate people"*.
- Face-to-face conversation is the most effective way of conveying information OR *"Face-to-face communications"*.
- The working software is the principal measure of progress OR *"Measure systems done"*.
- Agile processes promote sustainable development, the ability to maintain a constant pace OR *"Maintain sustainable pace"*.
- Good design and continuous attention to techno-functional excellence enhances agility OR *"Maintain design"*.
- Simplicity and continuous focus on % of work done rather than % of effort spent by team OR *"Keep it simple"*.

- Requirements, best architecture, and design emerge from all self-organizing teams OR *"Team creates architecture"*.
- Frequently reflect on how to improve efficiency OR *"Reflect and adjust"*.

Your description may vary, depending on what part of the principle stands out most for you, but the following are the possible abbreviations.

1.3 Key Agile Principles

- Focus on the customer and business value
- Iterative and fast development
- Flexible, adaptive, and continuously improving
- Collaboration and team work
- Empowered and self-directed teams

1.4 Agile Values

- **Trust:** Trust among the various stakeholders (team, scrum master, product owner, project manager) plays a vital role in making Agile successful.
- **Respect:** Individuals have to respect and consider the opinion of all the stakeholders, even if a team member is a fresher to the team.
- **Openness:** Team/scrum master should be open to the management and the product owner while providing the status updates, highlighting risks (both internal and external risks).
- **Courage:** Team should have the courage to say NO to the management if we cannot commit to the delivery with appropriate reasons.

What is Agile values?

Let's take a closer look at the Agile values together:

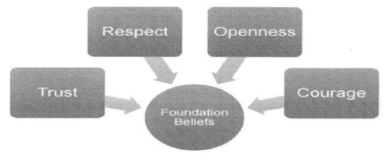

Figure 1.7: *Agile values (Image Source: https://www.scrumalliance.org)*

Your description may vary, depending on what part of the value stands out most for you/your customer/business, but these are the possible abbreviations.

What are your values?

"Your values are not just the values you practice, but the values you walk past"

~Australian General

1.5 Traditional Lifecycle Versus Agile Development

"Agile process is the universal remedy for software development project failure. Software applications developed through the Agile process have three times the success rate of the traditional Waterfall method and a much lower percentage of time and cost overruns."

- CHAOS Report, 2011 - Standish Group

Agile vs. Waterfall

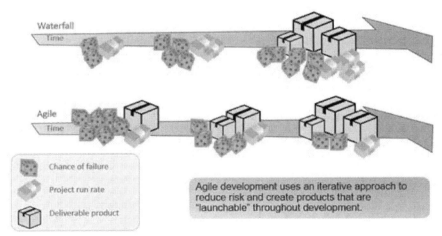

Figure 1.8: *Waterfall vs. Agile (Image Source: https://www.scrumalliance.org)*

According to the 2011 CHAOS report from the Standish Group, Agile projects are often more successful than non-Agile projects. The building blocks in the success of Agile process are:

- Capturing requirements through user stories
- Use of Agile Personas and wireframes
- Creating product roadmaps
- Story mapping

Predictive (Waterfall) Project Management

The waterfall or predictive method is the traditional way to manage projects for lead parts several decades. The waterfall method is very straightforward in its concept, as the project tasks are carried out in strict sequential order.

As part of planning, the project timeframe is split into a series of stages or phrases, with each one having a gate review at the end. This review is to check the progress and agree the plan for the next stage. Once approved, there is no going back! Just like a waterfall flowing down the hill.

These distinct endpoints or goals are set for each phase of development and cannot be revisited after completion. In this basic system, a team must complete one step before starting the next. Managers find this system very straightforward and easy-to-implement. The waterfall model emphasizes a logical progression of steps.

Just make a list of the task steps you need to accomplish a deliverable item and get to work! Team members can quickly understand waterfall processes, saving project managers valuable communication time.

The waterfall method is commonly used for projects of an industrial nature. Here, the task work is visible and stable. Once the plan has been approved, the project manager will use a *"command and control"* management approach and issue packages of work to the specialist team creating the products.

The construction industry is a good example of using the waterfall method. An architect's plan is created and agreed, and the project manager is there to oversee the construction. More managers use the Waterfall system than any other, and the process sequence usually follows the following stages or phases:

- Specification of consumer requirements
- Concept, design, and planning
- Creation of a physical product (construction, coding, etc.)
- Integration into current systems
- Validation (testing, debugging, etc.)
- Product installation
- Ongoing maintenance.

The Waterfall method best suits teams in manufacturing and construction that create physical products and follow precise assembly orders, and these plans from previous projects can be used as a template and applied to their current work with little or no adjustment.

The waterfall model is a linear, sequential approach to the software development life cycle that has been popular in software engineering and product development.

Before moving to the next stage or phase, there is usually a review and sign off process to ensure that all the defined goals (products/deliverables) have been met.

The waterfall approach is ideal for projects that have specific documentation, fixed requirements, ample resources, an established timeline, and well-understood technology. The waterfall method is composed of seven non-overlapping stages:

1. **Requirements:** Potential requirements, deadlines, and guidelines for the project are analyzed and placed into a functional specification. This stage handles the defining and planning of the project without mentioning specific processes.

2. **Analysis:** The system specifications are analyzed to generate product models and business logic that will guide production. This is also when financial and technical resources are audited for feasibility.

3. **Design:** A design specification document is created to outline technical design requirements like programming language, hardware, data sources, architecture, and services.

4. **Coding/Implementation:** The source code is developed using the models, logic, and requirements designated in the prior stages. Typically, the system is designed in smaller components or units before being implemented together.

5. **Testing:** This is when quality assurance, unit, system, and beta tests take place to report issues that may need to be resolved. This may cause a forced repeat of the coding stage for debugging. If the system passes the tests, the waterfall continues forward.

6. **Operation/deployment:** The product or application is deemed fully functional and is deployed to a live environment.

7. **Maintenance/support:** Corrective, adaptive, and perfective maintenance is carried out indefinitely to improve, update, and enhance the final product. This could include releasing patch updates or new versions.

However, there is a move toward using the Agile method (see later) for the development of software. Alternatives to the waterfall model include **Joint Application Development (JAD), Rapid Application Development (RAD),** sync-and-stabilize, **Agile Project Management (APM),** and the spiral model.

Waterfall Model Advantages

While agile or dynamic methods often replace the waterfall model, there are some advantages:

- Upfront documentation and planning stages allow for large or shifting teams to remain informed and move towards a common goal

- It forces a structured and disciplined organization
- It is simple to understand, follow, and sequence tasks
- Waterfall facilitates departmentalization and managerial control based on schedule or deadlines
- It reinforces good coding habits to define before design and then code
- Waterfall allows for early design or specification changes to be made easily
- Waterfall clearly defines milestones and deadlines

Disadvantages of the Waterfall Model

These are typically associated with the risk associated with a lack of revision, including:

- Design is not adaptive; often, the entire process needs to start over when a flaw is found
- It ignores the potential to receive mid-process user or client feedback and make changes based on the results
- Teams that need to change their plans as their projects progress, however, will find this method quite limiting
- Delays testing until the end of the development life cycle
- Does not consider error correction
- Does not handle requests for changes, scope adjustments, or updates well
- Reduces efficiency by not allowing processes to overlap
- No working product is available until the later stages of the life cycle The whenever do dollars away the answer project on your walk along
- Not ideal for complex, high risk, ongoing, or object-oriented projects.

Traditional projects start with a fixed scope and expand time and cost as needed to accomplish the work. In contrast, agile projects fix the time and cost and allow the scope to vary. This is the key difference between agile and traditional methods, as depicted below.

Agile vs. Waterfall – Triple Constraints

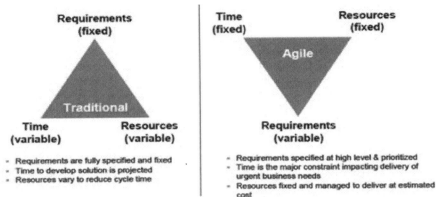

Figure 1.9: Waterfall vs. Agile – Triple constraints (Image Source: https://www.scrumalliance.org)

More product management than project management. Manage the delivery of features, not the use of time and resources.

Agile vs. Waterfall – High-level Comparison

Let's discuss the high-level key differences between Agile and waterfall:

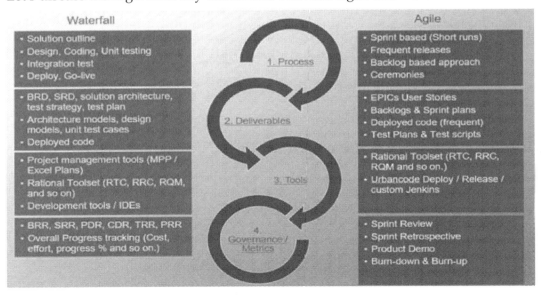

Figure 1.10: Waterfall vs. Agile – High-level comparison (Image Source: https://www.scrumalliance.org)

Agile development is mainstream, and even the US government is going agile.

Agile development is appropriate when you are developing a product/system in the face of uncertainty. Agile development flips the triangle of constraints to keep scope negotiable. It is approached in layers:

- Agile engineering
- Agile project management
- Agile product management
- Agile contracting

Agile engineering builds on a foundation of three practices:

- Continuous delivery
- Test-driven development
- Refactoring

1.6 How Agile Mapped to Traditional Practices

Let's discuss how we can map Agile phase(s) with traditional project phase(s), as consultant/practitioner often becomes biased in these:

Traditional	Agile
Defining	**Envisioning**
Defines and authorizes the project	Defines the product sufficiently to provide a sandbox with borders in which to work
Planning	**Roadmap**
Describes how the project will be managed	Translates the vision into a set of features and an expected timebox in which to deliver
Executing	**Release**
Helps the project groups work together to complete the work	Helps the team incrementally and iteratively develop potentially shippable code
Monitoring and Controlling	**Adapting**
Checks the progress of the project and corrects problems	Integrates planned stopping points to inspect and adapt the process and product
Closing	**Closing**
Formally closes each phase or the project and receives approval of the project work	Team reflects on achievements and decision-making per lessons learned

Integration Management	Agile Planning
Develop project charter or plan	Develop roadmap and backlog
Execute the project plan	Do iteration work
Direct, manage, monitor, control	Facilitate, lead, collaborate
Integrated change control	Constant feedback, ranked backlog
Scope and Time Management	Time Boxes
Collect requirements, define scope	Develop and select product backlog
Create Work Breakdown Structure (WBS)	Define features for release/sprint
Define and sequence activity	Team selects features, tasks for sprint
Control schedule	Refine story estimates per team velocity
Quality Management	Integrated quality
Quality Planning	Responsibility of entire team
Quality Assurance	QA integrated into sprints, retrospectives
Quality Control	Unit testing in each iteration
Human Resource Management	Self-managing teams
Human Resource Planning	Dedicated team of 7 +/- 2 members
Team Development	Cross-functional, collaborative teams
Team Management	Servant leadership, self-managing teams

Table 1.1: How Agile mapped to traditional practices

Your description may vary, depending on what part of the principle stands out most for you, but the above-mentioned are the possible abbreviations.

1.7 Agility Versus Agile

Agility: It is the property of an organization to sense and respond to market changes and continuously deliver value to customers.

Agile: An organizational approach and mindset defined by the values and principles of the Agile Manifesto, often practiced through a framework like Scrum.

1.8 The State of Agility

A vast majority of organizations recognize the importance of agility and its rewards. Yet, agility can be elusive: Many are struggling to translate this nearly 20-year-old software development strategy into a broader management concept. To successfully transform, today's organizations need to embrace agility from strategy to execution, enterprise-wide.

The time to do so is now. Our survey findings indicate that two-thirds (66%) of organizations have experienced less than 10% growth in revenue over the last fiscal year. Trends like this make the ability to react quickly to emerging trends, design better products, enhance team morale, and meet sky-high customer expectations more critical than ever.

Take a look at an illustration of the top benefits of organizational agility:

Figure 1.11: The top benefits of organizational agility (Image Source: Forbes insights)

Organizations already recognize the value of agility. A staggering 81% of all survey respondents consider it to be the most important characteristic of a successful organization. Also, 82% of the respondents consider agility to be extremely important to an organization's success and competitiveness. Among the most popular Agile approaches selected by respondents was Scrum, which was cited by more than three-quarters (77%) of leaders.

Let's take a look at the functions in which organizations are most Agile:

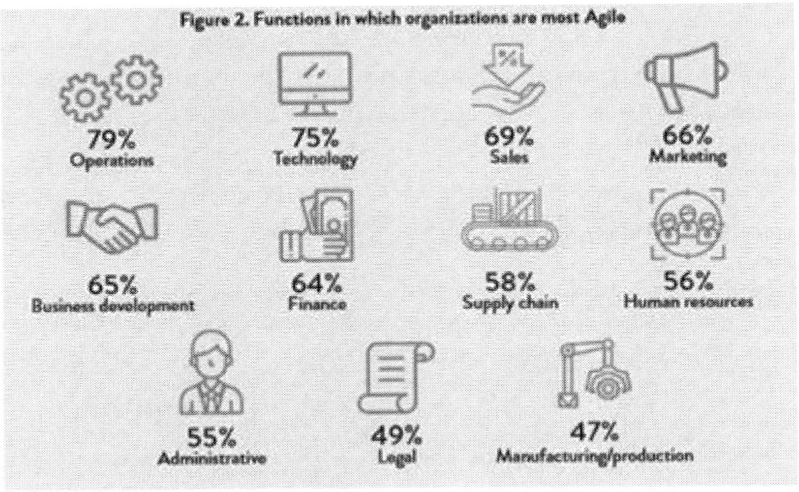

Figure 1.12: Functions in which organizations are most Agile (Image Source: Forbes insights)

Agility is a prerequisite to stay competitive in the long run; it is not optional, says *Joerg Erle* Meier, the Chief Operating Officer of Nokia, a Finnish multinational telecommunications and consumer electronics company. *Being Agile enables us to respond faster and better meet our customers' requests.* Agile initiatives at Nokia include redesigning business processes, creating a customer-centric supply chain, and introducing smaller, more nimble teams.

There's good reason for the popularity of organizational agility. For those that succeed at achieving greater agility, leaders and laggards see many benefits, including faster time-to-market, faster innovation, and improved non-financial results.

Toyota Motor Corporation is one of the companies reaping the benefits of increased agility. By working "*in small batches*" and creating continuous process flows like the Toyota Production System, Nigel Thurlow, the chief of Agile for Toyota Connected (the global technology strategy business unit for Toyota), says that the company's Kentucky manufacturing plant can upgrade systems that support the plant machinery in six days—a fraction of the seven weeks once required for the exact same task. "*When you're working in short sprints and small batches, you're able to see the value delivered more rapidly,*" he says. "*But more importantly, you're able to catch your mistakes more rapidly, change your mind and make decisions based upon emerging requirements.*"

Such flexibility is imperative in today's business environment, as the rapid pace of technology, innovation, and development requires organizations to deliver results faster than ever. That said, agility is about more than getting products out the door faster than your competitors. Agile began as a response to the failures of traditional software development. Faced with blown budgets and missed deadlines, organizations turned to Agile to increase the rate at which they could create new products and roll out updates.

Let's look at the types of approaches currently employed by leaders and laggards:

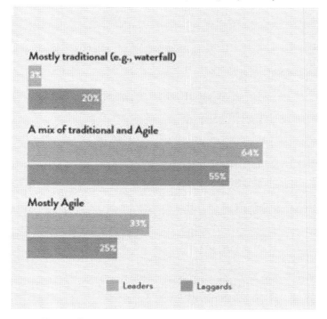

Figure 1.13: *Types of approaches currently employed by leaders and laggards*
(Image Source: Forbes insights)

Your description may vary, depending on what part of the principle stands out most for you, but the above-mentioned are possible abbreviations.

1.9 Three Steps to Increase Agility

Let's understand the three key steps to increase agility:

1. Create a C-suite with an Agile mindset
2. Hire and develop the right mix of talent
3. Foster an Agile-friendly culture and organizational structure

These strategies enable organizations, many of which are being upended by innovation, to expand agility throughout the organization for sustainable business growth and transformation success. Solving a client's issue may require many complex work streams, so we set up a sprint. It's a way of getting people to be collaborative, take accountability, and feel empowered.

-- TAMARA INGRAM CHIEF EXECUTIVE OFFICER,
J. WALTER THOMPSON COMPANY

1.10 Agile Framework

There are over a dozen actively-used agile methodologies. The most common approaches are Scrum, Extreme Programming (XP), lean product development, Kanban, SAFe, the Dynamic Systems Development Method (DSDM), and the Crystal family of methods.

Agile Framework

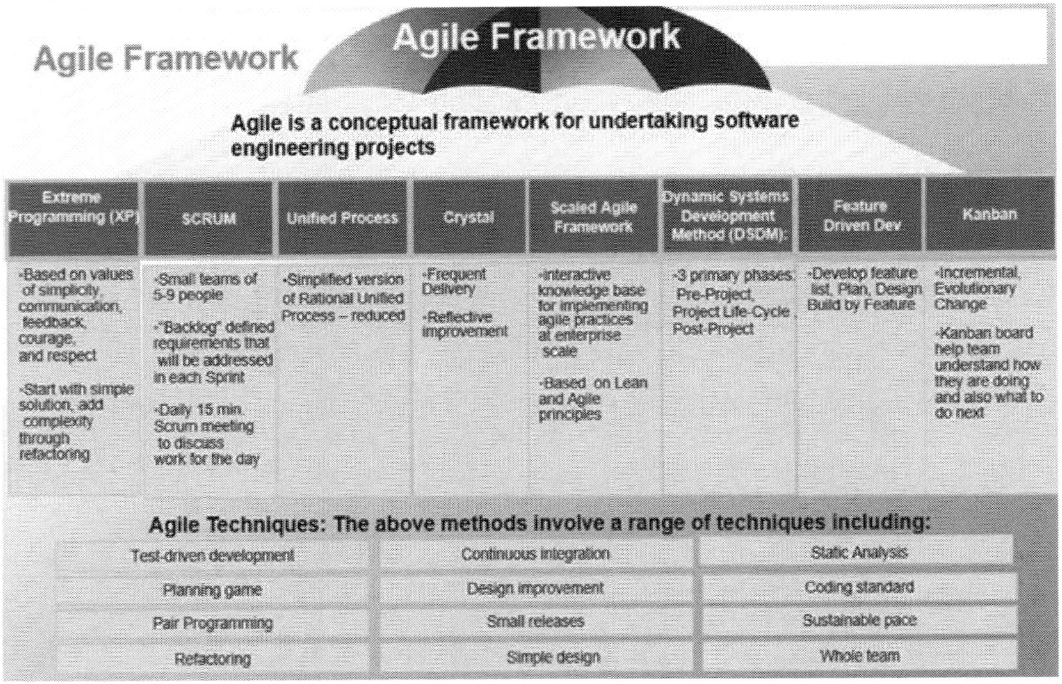

Figure 1.14: *Agile framework (Image Source: https://www.scrumalliance.org)*

Agile methodology encourages the continuous iteration of advancement and testing during the project software development life cycle. Here are some Agile frameworks that can be implemented within Agile projects:

1. Extreme programming
2. Crystal methodologies
3. Scrum
4. Lean software development
5. Feature-driven development
6. Dynamic software development methods

Extreme programming is the successful method of developing Agile software, and it focuses on customer satisfaction. To develop the software, extreme programming requires maximum interaction with customers. It divides the entire software development life cycle into short growth sequences.

1.11 Agile Concepts

The core ideas of Agile are:

- **Adaptive:** The process and the team must be flexible
- **Iterative:** Agile development introduces efficient products in stages, which are evolving sets of completed and working software
- **People-oriented:** The organization should support teams and people, as they are essential elements for the success of a project

1.12 Benefits of Agile

Let's discuss some of the benefits of Agile:

- Empirical (relies on observation and experience)
- Lightweight (that makes it easy to understand but hard to master; Scrum is flexible and easy to deploy)
- Adaptive
- Fast but never hurried
- Exposes wastefulness
- Customer-centric
- Pushes decision making to lower levels
- Fosters trust, honesty, and courage
- Encourages self-organization
  - o Speed to market
  - o Right product
  - o Quality
  - o Flexibility
  - o Transparency
  - o Risk management
  - o Cost control

Let's explore the benefits of Agile:

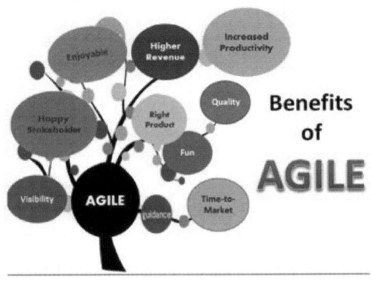

Figure 1.15: Benefits of Agile (Image source: https://www.prepaway.com/)

Agile training and certification help practitioners enhance their skill sets by interaction.

1.13 Agile Contracts Nuts and Bolts

Introduction

The goal of agile contracts is to enable close cooperation between the project team and the business or customer. This cooperation helps redirect the team's efforts towards delivering value-added features. This is also evident from the third value statement of the Agile Manifesto, which states "Customer collaboration over contract negotiation." An agile approach requires more trust between the parties than a traditional approach; it focuses on what resources are trying to build rather than bogging them down on debates about how changes will be negotiated or what the completion criteria is.

An agile approach also requires the business to be more involved in providing feedback on iterations, reprioritizing the backlog, and evaluating the value of change requests against the remaining work items. If there is a trust factor in place, agile contracts can be a great tool for extracting more value for the clients, so they have a competitive advantage. However, when the trust factor is absent, agile contracts will be a difficult buy in and may not be suitable as well.

What is required to build an Agile contract?

The key element of building an agile contract is a mindset. The following table can help understand the type of mindset shift expected from different stakeholders:

Stakeholder(s)	Traditional mindset	Agile mindset
Sales	Let's do whatever it takes to get the bid.	Let's not focus just on getting new customers, let's create happy ones too.
Procurement	We must know exactly what, when, and how much and have a discount.	There is a value in collaborative relationships and mutual motivation.
	We want the cheapest price.	We get what we pay for.
Legal	Let's reduce our risks and ensure that we don't suffer if things go wrong.	Agile can lower the risk, and there are existing models to support it.
Architects	Let's create the design upfront to meet our deadlines.	Let's keep our design options open until feasible.
Program management	Let's reduce risk by having phase gate milestones to check the progress.	Let's measure progress with working software, how much business value has been achieved, and how much risk has reduced.

Table 1.2: What is required to build an Agile contract

Your description may vary, depending on what part of the principle stands out most for you, but the above-mentioned are possible abbreviations.

Principles of Agile Contracts

Let's discuss how we can adapt the principles of Agile contracts:

Principle	Focus on	Results in
Alignment of incentives	Pay for outcomes, not for effort Responsive to changes	Encourage vendors to create value
	Sharing benefits of continuous improvement	Have ability to update scope
		Have rewards for vendors demonstrating efficiency

Collaboration and transparency	Maintaining trust Focus on vision and not process	Assume that parties act in good faith Clear goals/objectives in contract and reference backlog for detailed scope
Ability to inspect and adapt	Establish regular feedback cycles Set the rules of engagement Anticipate the unexpected	Specify Sprint cycle and review, retrospectives, and backlog refinement meetings Identify roles & processes to give feedback, refine backlog, accept work Define how likely extensions of initial contract will be handled.

Table 1.3: Principles of Agile contracts

We've said that agile is a mindset and not a specific set of practices, and many agile teams end up tailoring their agile methodology to their own circumstances.

Let's look at some sample sections of a contract:

Section	Example
Period of performance	2-week sprints, until ended by either party
Engagement resources	A Dev team in the Philippines with a scrum master & business analyst A customer product owner to answer any questions
Scope of work	Clear goals for the first threee sprints (proof of concept) After that, contract backlog will define scope
Client & vendor responsibilities	Client provides feedback & maintains prioritized backlog Vendor provides transparency and demo after every sprint
Fee schedule	Vendor is paid at the end of each 1-week sprint
Termination/ renewal	Both parties can decide to renew or cancel after each sprint review

Table 1.4: Some sample sections of a contract

Time and Material (T&M) contracts are a good fit for Agile engagements.

Fixed Price/Fixed Capacity (FPFC) contract is most suitable for Agile, whereas a contract with fixed price/fixed scope must be avoided.

We have noticed that most clients know only a small percentage of their complete requirements at the start of a new project. This is more so for an application/site development, and we observed something very similar in platform/technology migration situations as well. Later, most customers wanted to add new features as well, which makes it somewhat like new development. Asking them to define the priorities is almost impossible, so we have tried various things here (in case of fixed price).

For risk & impact/analyse and design phase, we have put T&M contract, for build & testing till UAT, we have put fixed price – 70/30 mode, which puts 30% of the revenue on a penalty mode if there is any slippage in timeline or quality. Closely work with client to create contract, which includes defining the prerequisites and exit criteria. After UAT till Go-Live and support/hyper-care phase, we have put T&M contract.

Reference – Visit the following URL for a detailed case study:

https://www.linkedin.com/pulse/agile-scrum-contract-best-practices-sudipta-malakar-csp/

1. We try and explain that any changes to the requirements will swap out an equal sized but lower-priority requirement. So, the client keeps the budget in check and has flexibility even late in the project life cycle to add/remove requirements.

2. We try and have a T&M requirement phase where the product backlog is frozen (maybe 80%) and then give a fixed bid quote (with appropriate assumptions and margins for error).

3. We have clauses in the contract where we say that project estimates will be revisited at specified intervals and all estimations etc. will be transparent.

While these measures have helped, it really depends a lot on the client's understanding of Agile and their willingness to collaborate. Otherwise, it's always a tough and bumpy ride, especially in Agile projects.

Different Types of Agile Contracts

Let's discuss the different types of agile contracts and some tips & tricks:

Figure 1.16: Different types of Agile contracts (Image Source: PMI PMBOK)

Other popular contract types include paying by features contract, time and materials contract, fixed price and fixed scope contract, and fixed profit contract.

Contract - Illustration

Let's check out an illustration of contract:

Thorup and Jensen (2009) explain in their paper the option of Graduated Fixed Price (see Exhibit3)

Project Completion	Total Fee	Graduated Rate
Finish Early	$87,000	$117/hour
Finish On-Time	$100,000	$100/hour
Finish Late	$113,000	$90/hour

Figure 1.17: Contract – Illustration (Image Source: PMI PMBOK)

We've said that agile is a mindset and not a specific set of practices, and many agile teams end up tailoring their agile methodology to their own circumstances.

Conclusion

No contract can make us agile, but a bad contract will stop us from becoming agile and compromise the benefits that both parties can gain from agility.

Agile Contracts - Modeling a Transformation in Contracting

Introduction to Contracts

Business dictionary definition of a 'Contract' is: A voluntary, deliberate, and legally binding agreement between two or more competent parties. A contractual relationship is evidenced by an offer, an acceptance of the offer, and a valid (legal and valuable) consideration. Each party to a contract acquires rights and duties relative to the rights and duties of the other parties. While all parties may expect a fair benefit from the contract (otherwise courts may set it aside as inequitable), it does not follow that each party will benefit to an equal extent.

Any contract is defined by the level of risk each party involved is willing to accept. This involves three fundamental points to consider in contracting:

1. What is the cost/budget?
2. What is the duration/time estimate?
3. What are the deliverables or what is the scope?

Traditional contracts that were used in the industry are: fixed-price contract where the payment amount does not depend on resources used or time expended, and Time and Material (T&M) contract wherein billing clients happens for actual work scope based on the hourly rates of labor. Customers are charged for the number of hours spent on a specific project, plus the cost of the materials consumed.

Among the traditional ones, the T&M contract is the most commonly used when it comes to compatibility with agile methods where the project scope is not yet fully known, and we have flexibility to modify the scope or vary the workloads as and when needed.

Capped T&M involves a cap on the price a customer needs to pay for the supplier, and it is also a subset of T&M. 'Fixed' contracts are not suitable for agile, as the trust level between the parties is generally low.

Fixed contracts include:

1. Fixed cost but flexible scope and time
2. Fixed time but flexible scope and time
3. Fixed cost and time but flexible scope
4. Fixed cost and scope but flexible time
5. Fixed time and scope but flexible cost

Triple Constraints

Another key difference between the agile mindset and traditional project management is the agile or "inverted" triangle of constraints. This triangle, illustrated in the following figure, was introduced in the first edition of the DSDM Manual, published in 1994.

This reversal of the traditional triangle means that agile teams allow the scope to vary within the fixed parameters of cost and time. In other words, we aim to deliver the most value we can by X date within X budget. Although we'll begin with a high-level vision of the end product, we can't define how much we'll be able to get done upfront; that will emerge as we move closer to the target date.

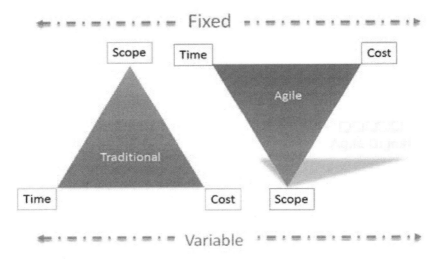

Figure 1.18: Triple constraints (Image source: https://www.scrumalliance.org)

Creating Agile Contracts

When we think about agile contracts, we must consider the agile manifesto statement: *"Customer collaboration over contract negotiation"*. This essentially means that we must try and create a trust level between the parties involved in the contract to create a collaboration that facilitates agility and focuses on outcomes rather than output.

Agile contracts are incremental delivery contracts, which mean that there is always a flexibility to both the parties to retrospect and part ways at regular prescribed points of time if the association is not providing the expected results.

Incremental means that they are as frequent as 2 weeks to 4 weeks as and when a team delivers to the customer. If the relationship is new between both the parties and the trust level is low, as in the pyramid of trust, we may start with fixed contracts.

Pyramid of Trust

Let's discuss the different types of tips & tricks of the "*Pyramid of Trust*":

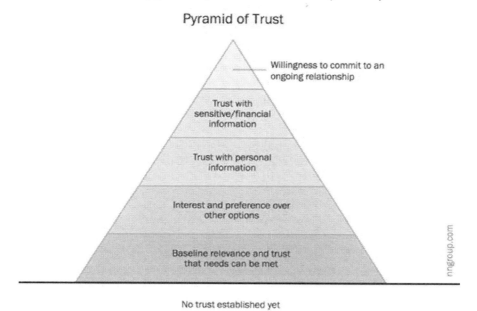

Figure 1.19: *Pyramid of trust (Image reference: nngroup.com)*

Ideally, we may negotiate and start with a fixed time and cost but flexible scope contract for a Minimum Viable Product (MVP). During the execution of the project and incremental delivery retrospectives, both parties may move from baseline relevance to interest in each other and preference over other suppliers.

MVP to product/service development partnership takes a few consistent 'Fixed time and cost but flexible with scope' associations between two parties. At this stage, the trust level will be that of both parties sharing personal and financial information under non-disclosure agreements.

Moving to Outcome-based Partnerships

True '*Trusted supplier*', '*Outsource partner*' tags require a supplier to start with 'routine' work and' *Focused* 'work contracts to prove their capability and resilience before starting out with '*Leverage*,' where both parties understand and work to their strengths, and finally, to strategic alliances.

Value Risk Matrix

Let's discuss the different types of tips & tricks of "*Value Risk Matrix*":

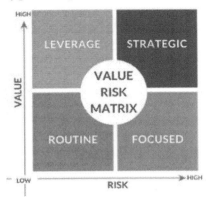

Figure 1.20: *Value Risk Matrix (Image source: https://www.axelos.com)*

Strategic and operational agility of both parties is an important factor for the success of any outcome-based partnerships. For example, both the supplier and customer organizations may use **Objectives and Key Results (OKRs)** in building operational sync and common measures of success of partnership in working - collaborating teams.

Outcome-based contracting requires us to focus beyond the output/deliverables on the business outcome and creating win-win situations.

Traditional Contract vs. Outcome-based Contract

Let's discuss the different types of contract tips & tricks:

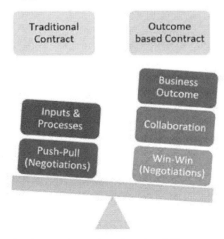

Figure 1.21: *Traditional contract vs. outcome based contract (Image source: https://www.axelos.com)*

'Rolls Royce - Power by hour' and 'GE aviation- True Choice Flight hour' are two good examples of outcome-based business contracts.

Challenges to Adoption of Outcome-based Model

- Developing a common measurement and analysis system to agree on measures and metrics by both service provider/supplier and customer is the primary challenge.
- The second challenge is the mindset or cultural shift needed from both parties.
- Letting go of the control of people and process to the supplier from the customer.

Both parties should be able to quantify the risk of the engagement and move towards common business goals.

Overcoming Challenges

Setting up a core team at leadership level facilitated by external executive coach/ consultant to create a workshop for defining the rules and boundaries of engagement would be a starting step.

The focus shall be on transparency of business opportunities and challenges, and flexibility in choosing pricing models based on the business situations, expected outcomes (refer to the risk model), and the predictability of expected business outcomes and profits. This includes defining both strategic and operational outcomes with common method of measurement, i.e., KRA/KPIs at the operational level.

The second step is to define OKRs for people at working level for working agreements.

Conclusion

Moving from low-trust competition to high-trust partnership and co-creation will need significant investment in transformation of leadership and workforce from a closed- to open-system thinking.

The Co-creation Transition Model

Let's depict "*The co-creation transition model*". We live in VUCA times — volatile, uncertain, complex, and ambiguous. Those were the words the US Military began to organize around at the turn of the century, and they easily describe the world in which we live today. New Stories has developed a six-stage spiral, a map for navigating difficult times and co-creating the results we wish to see:

1. Listen for the opening/change
2. Name the possibility/shift

3. Connect the innovators

4. Nourish the system

5. Co-create results

6. Illuminate new stories

The Co-creation Transition Model

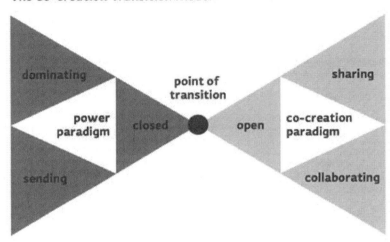

Figure 1.22: The co-creation transition model (Image source: https://www.axelos.com)

Your description may vary, depending on what part of the principle stands out most for you, but the above-mentioned are possible abbreviations. We've said that agile is a mindset and not a specific set of practices, and many agile teams end up tailoring their agile methodology to their own circumstances.

1.15 Backlog Management in Agile

Product and solution requirements in various agile practices are being managed through a list of prioritized requirements called backlog. Backlogs help align the business priorities with the priorities of engineering teams. A common backlog for a product ensures that the teams are always working on the highest priority requirements that maximize the business value delivered by the team. So, they help create a common focus for all the members of the development team.

Backlog gets refined and re-prioritized at different stages by stakeholders before the development teams start working on it. As the backlog is refined at each of these stages, requirements can be identified more clearly. This may result in addition of more items to backlog. Additional requirements can also be identified based on team specific needs, and they help the teams deliver more efficiently and improve quality.

Depending on the stage of development or delivery and stakeholders, backlog can be of the following three types:

- Portfolio backlog
- Program backlog
- Product backlog

Portfolio Backlog

Portfolio backlog contains several initiatives. These features are prioritized based on their business criticality relative to each other, the vision of the organization, and market trends. Some initiatives are also added to explore technical enhancements to support future development efforts. Any technical debt items to be worked on at the organizational level are added to the list and relatively prioritized with other initiatives. As we learn more about changes in customer and market expectations, more initiatives can be added to the portfolio back, and priorities need to be re-adjusted.

Portfolio backlog is maintained and updated by customer facing executives who have an understanding of the organization's business, financial, and technical context. They ensure that investment is aligned to business priorities of the organization and in line with its vision.

In order to prioritize the initiatives, we need to understand the business value provided by them. Initiatives are prioritized relative to each other and sized at a high level (small, medium, large, extra large, etc.). If an initiative is too large or complex, other initiatives are added for studying it and bring clarity. This brings out dependencies and highlights the risks that would have been hidden otherwise.

There could be multiple independent ongoing initiatives in the organization. Although it is desirable that these initiatives be completely independent, there could be some dependencies since they are part of the same product or solution. To create a valuable solution, it is important to understand these dependencies and create a valuable solution/product for customers. Initiatives might need to be re-prioritized to create a solution when we understand these dependencies. Business and technical leaders responsible for these initiatives coordinate among themselves and prioritize the work to ensure that dependencies are taken care of.

Program Backlog

In order to accomplish the initiatives in portfolio, smaller and more manageable features are added in the program backlog. The product management team is responsible for program backlog. Collaboration with customers, customer facing teams and engineering teams enables product management to add features to the program backlog. These features are prioritized based on the value they deliver. If there are technical debts at program level, they are added to the backlog as well and prioritized along with the features. Any significant architectural changes needed for the upcoming features are also prioritized as features in the product backlog. Plus, dependencies on features from other initiatives are also considered when prioritizing the features.

Program backlog refinement occurs between two releases when feature development is in progress. Items in the program backlog need to be actively and continuously managed to align with market and customer needs. Priority and value created by features is assessed during interactions with customers, customer facing teams, and product evangelists. Based on these interactions, new features are created and prioritized. If lower priority features don't provide the desired ROI, development is stopped.

Any large feature is broken down into smaller features, such that each broken down feature can be completed within a release and creates value for the customer. Acceptance criteria are added for the features to determines when the feature is considered complete. It is important to allocate time for technical debts and architectural features along with the customer features so that the team can continue to develop customer at a sustainable pace. In order to have a balance between the three, a fixed proportion of each of these is agreed upon and the capacity of the team is planned accordingly. Based on this assessment, draft release content is formed. Release content is created for the subsequent two releases. It is then reviewed and adjusted based on new facts known at the start of the release in which it needs to be worked on.

Commitments for requirements planned for the long term are not considered firm. Since the requirement is planned for long term, there is some uncertainty. A team might need to work on other higher-priority requirement than the long-term one. In such a case, it will be difficult product management to manage the customer.

Product Backlog

Product backlog contains user stories required to build the feature in program backlog. It also contains user stories that a team creates based on discussions and action items created in a retrospective meeting. User stories related to technical debt, which enable the team to work more efficiently, are also created and added to the product backlog.

Product owner is responsible for creating and managing the product backlog. SMEs and members of other leadership team negotiate with the product owner to add user stories related to technical debt and prioritize them. Based on the value these technical debt user stories will add to enhance the capability of the team, they are prioritized along with user stories with create customer features. Product owner identifies the part product backlog that can be accomplished in a sprint and the business objective that would be met through it. Product owner also considers the capacity of the team when doing so.

During the sprint or development phase, the development team allocates some time (max 10% according to the Scrum guide) for grooming user stories for subsequent sprints. Feature is broken into more user stories, and details are added to the new and existing ones. User stories are prioritized to deliver early business value to customers. User stories are estimated at a high level, and those of higher priority have more details and clarity of scope and are ready to be taken-up in the next 1-2 sprints. User stories of lower priority have less detail. More details are added as more is learnt about the feature scope, or user stories are dropped if they don't create the desired value.

If product development is using the Scrum framework, user stories are discussed, and the team learns more about them during sprint planning. This discussion between the team and product owner is important as the team learns more about customer expectations through it. Based on this discussion, new user stories are identified, and details are added to them and previous user stories initially created by the product owner. Based on the facts that have been uncovered in the sprint planning meeting, the team estimates the user stories again. It takes up high-priority user stories for the sprint that they can complete and deliver value to customer. If user stories cannot be taken up in the Sprint, they are sent back to the product backlog to be prioritized in the next Sprint.

Conclusion

Backlog is refined at different stages by different people based on their area of expertise, the exposure to products, and the customers they have. A common backlog keeps the team and organization focused on a common goal. Let's summarize the different types of backlogs and stakeholders responsible for them:

The key element of building an agile contract is a mindset. The following table can help understand the backlog refinement expected from different stakeholders:

Backlog type	Content	Stakeholder responsible
Portfolio backlog	Initiatives	Executives
Program backlog	Features	Product management
Product backlog	User stories	Product owner

Table 1.5: Backlog refinement – Stakeholders responsible

Backlogs are primarily focused on creating customer value. Some backlog items are added to experiment and get more clarity on features or the approach to be taken for development. Backlog also contains some content that will help the team become more efficient (technical debt-related action items from retrospective meeting etc.).

1.16 Role of Manager (People) in an Agile Organization

In Agile organizations, members are self-organized, empowered teams and are constantly learning new skills from each other. A *"Product Owner"* prioritizes the team's task and organizes and manages the product backlog. A *"Scrum Master"* removes impediments and escalates issues to ensure that team productivity and quality remains high. So, there is no specific role called project manager. Are managers soon to be an endangered species in this world of agile?

Today, most agile organizations are doing things in a more responsible manner, and they're doing them without managers. Now the question is, "Where do managers fit in, in this type of culture?"

Managers using old methodology can limit both the productivity of the team and the power of agile. While managing in a way that builds self-organization can be a challenge, getting rid of managers isn't the solution to boosting productivity. At the same time, the traditional approach to the management role needs to change. What we're seeing is the rise of a more skilled form of management. A manager's prime focus shouldn't be to manage but to help and facilitate, motivate, and coach the team. In other words, what growing organizations need are leaders, not managers.

Redefine your role:
- Empowering over command
- Transparency over privacy
- Network over hierarchies
- Experimental over planning

Empowering Over Command

Traditional management often relies more on command rather than influence. For agile teams, the opposite needs to be true. Using influence can often be more effective in the long term for any organization, but it's essential on an agile team. A command culture can hinder a team's ability to develop self-organizational skills, which are at the heart of the value that agile brings to an organization.
- **Traditional:** Assigning individual to-do lists
- **Agile:** Empowering the team with skills

Transparency Over Privacy

The traditional approach, the project manager is holding the helm of the project, so others don't get to make decisions. In agile methodology, everything is transparent, and the clients and decision makers are actively involved in the initiation, planning, review, and testing of a product.

- **Traditional:** Others have no say in decision making
- **Agile:** Transparency plays a significant role in constituting a healthy Agile environment

Network Over Hierarchies

In networked organizations, people work in a self-managed way. Managers have become enablers of self-managing teams and networks rather than controllers of individuals.

- **Traditional:** Organizing work through authority
- **Agile:** Organizing work through mutual understanding

Experimental Over Planning

An agile mindset understands that failure is natural and builds a home for improvement. Also, early failure is like a cherry on the cake, as it teaches us what does and doesn't work in the early stages itself. It also recognizes that there is no clear path to success and innovation and the team has to find its way through constant experimentation and adapting to a new way of looking at the problem. In traditional management, failure is not seen as an option, so there is no easy way to deal with it.

- **Traditional:** Fixed scope
- **Agile**: Empirical mind-set, flexible scope

What do Agile managers do?

1. The manager becomes a facilitator and change agent/servant and leader/ chaos controller.
2. Coaching Agile teams – Creating Agile teams is one thing and having them follow agile effective is another. In other words, leading and coaching the team becomes significantly important.
3. Managing budgets.
4. Recruiting.
5. Setting expectations – Benchmarking and monitoring expectations by carrying out periodic reviews.
6. Putting out fires – As the manager, it's your responsibility to resolve all conflicts and put the team on a smooth track without hampering productivity.
7. A manager can work as an Agile coach, a scrum master, a product owner, or a DEV team member based on the business needs.

Overall, I don't see mangers getting extinct; we just need to put the cap of agility to redefine their role. Agile managers can help the team thrive, but management can have an adverse effect without proper guidance about what it means to be a manager in an agile organization.

1.17 Agile Estimation and Planning at Program and Portfolio Level

Is there any relation between estimation and commitment? Absolutely not; estimation is an approximate calculation, an educated guess, a prediction of a quantity, amount, extent, or value of something. On the other hand, commitment is the willingness to give your time and energy to something that you believe in, or it refers to a promise or firm decision to do something. Now, is there a relation between estimation and forecasting? Definitely yes; forecasting is to predict or estimate (a future event or trend).

In project teams, estimation is often considered a commitment for which teams start spending too much time to get details for accurate estimates. For one such reason, the 2011 Scrum Guide has removed the term "commit" in favor of "forecast" in regard to the work selected for a Sprint.

Estimations are based on experience and information available at our disposal at that time, with a known fact that all factors pertaining to our prediction or projection are either unclear or unknown. However, when other factors such as cost, time, business value, and time-to-market step in, estimates should become more accurate and contribute to the business's success. In other words, estimation at every instance of a project, from the task level till the release, decides the fate of a project and the business at large.

Estimations are more difficult to deal with in Agile projects, where requirements evolve dynamically, schedules are nailed down, scope is volatile, stakes are high, and teams are distributed. Also, estimates set expectations and if the outcome varies either with time or with respect to features, it will result in losses that have a magnified effect. So, besides being empirical, estimations in the agile world should be evolving and adaptive.

Advocates of classical estimation methods such as **Function Point Analysis (FPA)** might take this empirical approach with a pinch (or a bunch!) of salt. While classical estimation methods need well-defined requirements and try to reduce the possibility of uncertainty, Agile methodologies nurture change requests as important challenges, readily accept uncertainty, and try to address it by moving in a diametrically opposite direction. Traditional estimating approaches follow a "big-bang" task-based approach where the managers/leads develop a work breakdown structure with a list of tasks representing all the features. Then, they estimate the hours each task would possibly consume. Once done, these estimates are considered final and don't necessarily change throughout the project. However, the actual effort will change, and the rest of the project is spent adjusting and bridging the gap between the estimated and actual hours.

On the other hand, Agile estimations, are feature-based with a focus on the relative size of the prioritized features where the team comes up with an initial estimate and gets started with the objective of presenting a working product or prototype to the client immediately. The estimations are adjusted accordingly as the project progresses and more clarity emerges on the features. And as time progresses, each iteration should imbibe and incorporate the lessons learnt from previous iterations and releases, creating self-correcting, self-regulating estimates that are based in reality. Such reality-based estimations enable clients to continuously monitor the course of the projects, providing timely feedback and equipping the teams to constantly correct their plans and estimates.

Agile Estimating and Planning at Portfolio Level

This illustrates the Agile portfolio planning process (or portfolio management), which is an activity for determining which products or projects to work on, in which order, and for how long. The reality is that agile portfolio planning is a never-ending activity. As long as a company has products to develop or maintain, it has a portfolio to manage. Portfolio planning has two outputs: a portfolio backlog and a set of active products. A portfolio backlog is similar to a product backlog; but a product backlog contains items relevant to only one product, while a portfolio backlog describes multiple products, programs, or projects for which development has been approved but not yet begun. Each portfolio backlog item in the portfolio backlog might be a product, a product increment (one release of a product), or a project.

When estimating the size of portfolio backlog items, organizations should look for accuracy, not precision, because they will have a limited amount of data when these initial estimates are made. An effective and quick way to accurately predict product size is to use the T-shirt size estimates. T-shirt sizing is based on the concept of binning. The bins are typically assigned labels corresponding to those commonly used with T-shirt sizes: extra small, small, medium, large, extra-large, etc. Frequently, a cost range is associated with each size (e.g., an extra small project will cost between $10k and $25k) to provide organization-specific meaning to each T-shirt size. These measurements are accurate enough for decision making but not so precise as to be wasteful and most likely wrong.

Agile Estimating and Planning at Program/ Product Level

In Agile environments, plans evolve progressively, and so should estimates. We have features or requirements that need to be estimated starting from project, release, and at sprint levels. Agile methodologies employ a simple and effective technique of expressing a requirement as a *"user story"*.

Each user story has a different level of significance either in terms of time, cost, value, or convenience. User stories will be listed down in the product backlog and, the team starts picking them up in the order of priority, starting from the highest, and start planning and estimating them.

Estimations occur and change throughout projects, depending on the situation at hand. Teams need to do some initial estimating because at the beginning of iteration, they need to indicate what they think they're going to deliver (user stories picked up for that iteration), how they're going to do it (task breakdown from user stories), and how long they think it will take (about an epic spanning across iterations). Due to the inherent uncertainty in the information at the beginning of a project, we'll need to give *"ranged"* answers at first and then tighten up the answers as the project progresses.

In Agile, we follow a simple rule: people who will do the work (the development team) collectively provide the estimates. As everyone on the development team sees the story from a different perspective, it's essential that all members participate during estimation.

Relative Size Estimation

This estimates user stories/PBIs using relative sizes, not absolute sizes. In other words, it determines how large each item is relative to others. People are much more accurate at gauging relative measures (e.g., halfway there or a one-third) than they are at absolute measures (e.g., 10 feet or 6 kgs).

Story Points

Story points are a unit of measure for expressing an estimate of the overall effort that will be required to fully implement a product backlog item or any other piece of work. When we estimate with story points, we assign a point value to each item. The raw values we assign are unimportant; what matters are the relative values. A story that is assigned a 2 should be twice as much as a story that is assigned a 1. It should also be two-thirds of a story that is estimated as 3 story points. **Planning Poker** helps size the PBIs in story points.

As story points represent the effort to develop a story, a team's estimate must include everything that can affect the effort. That could include:

- The amount of work to do
- The complexity of the work
- Any risk or uncertainty in doing the work
- The definition of done

Ideal Days

An alternative approach for measuring PBIs is to use ideal days—the number of effort-days or person-days needed to complete a story. Ideal time is not the same as elapsed time. A football game would be measured as 60 minutes in ideal time (4, 15-minute quarters), but the elapsed time is closer to 3.5 to 4 hours. The main drawback of ideal time is that it can be misinterpreted as elapsed time, which leads to confusion and frustration.

Conclusion

Often, teams transitioning to agile find it hard to switch from the traditional task-based predictive estimates to feature-based speculative estimates and question the benefit in making a painful transition. As estimations set expectations, the teams might experience hiccups initially, but estimations become more pragmatic and accurate as the sprints or iterations progress. So, estimations can help teams make significant decisions, get a better understanding of stories, and gain an insight on design and architectural directions in future. There's no fixed time or short cuts defined for the teams to get better at estimations. Each team's approach to estimation evolves as the project progresses; they might struggle at first but then can get quite good at it, and they may probably reach a point where they often don't need it as higher trust levels lead to lesser estimation effort.

1.18 Agile Budget Management

Agile budget calculation is hot buzzword now. Here, you need to calculate your labor costs, non-labor costs, and NFR costs in addition to calculating your labor costs for functional/technical requirements.

How is your budget being allocated today?

- Top-down decision by leader/leaders
- The same budget as last year with small changes
- Start from scratch each year by aligning resources to priorities
- I don't know

SCRUM – Common Challenges

Let's depict some of the common Scrum challenges today:

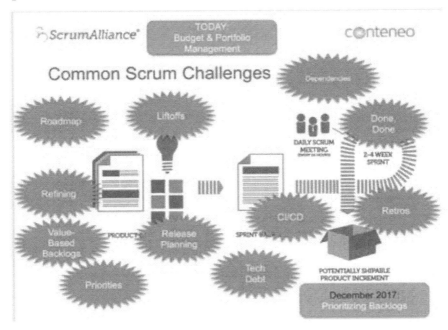

Figure 1.23: SCRUM – Common challenges (Image source: https://www.scrumalliance.org)

In Agile, we are getting big business requirements in terms of Epics, which are combinations of related user stories.

- Prepare and estimate the project requirements using planning poker
- Determine the team's velocity

Calculation of Velocity Per Sprint - Example

Velocity - The work completed within a given time period, usually an iteration or sprint, used to plan and estimate the team's capacity. Estimation in Scrum is based on what's called Velocity.

Velocity is a measure of how much product backlog the team can complete in a given amount of time.

Velocity is a long-term measure that indicates how much work is "done" per sprint. It is the number of points completed per sprint. Partially finished stories don't count, and it varies in every sprint:

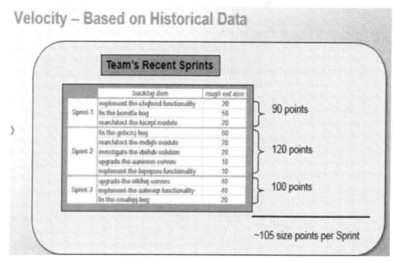

Figure 1.24: Calculation of velocity per sprint - Example

How do we know team's velocity?

If the team is in place for some time, look at the history of the team's velocity. If the team is new, run a couple of sprints to establish the initial velocity. Use the average velocity over several sprints to predict the completion date.

Different Types of Planning in SCRUM

Scrum has five primary planning activities, or planning games: vision planning, roadmap planning, release planning, iteration planning, and daily planning, as depicted below:

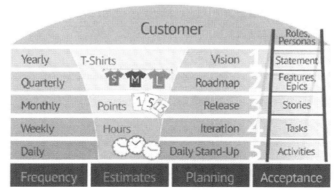

Figure 1.25: Different types of planning in SCRUM (Image source: https://www.scrumalliance.org)

Reference – Go to the following URL for a detailed case study:

https://www.linkedin.com/pulse/agile-budget-calculation-utopia-worldwide-across/

1.19 Managing Bottlenecks with Kanban

A process bottleneck interrupts the flow of work and causes delays across the production process. It is a work stage that gets more work requests than it can process at its maximum throughput capacity.

1.19.1 What Is a Bottleneck?

Let's look at some key pointers on bottleneck definition:

- Capacity Constrained Resources (CCR)
- Small staff for testing and deployment
- Lack of operational maturity
- Inconsistent environments
- Technical debts
- Non-Instant Availability (NIA)
- Product owner availability
- Dependency on third party
- Management approval
- Legacy business process

1.19.2 Five Focusing Steps to Increase Throughput

Let's look at some key pointers to increase throughput:

- Identify the system's constraint(s)
- Decide how to exploit the system's constraint(s)
- Subordinate everything else to the above decision(s)
- Elevate the system's constraint(s)
- Start all over!

1.19.3 Exploit the Bottleneck

Let's look at some key pointers to exploit the bottleneck:

- Exploiting means we are ensuring that the bottleneck isn't distracted by non-throughput producing work.

- Ensure that the bottleneck always works on the highest priority, highest-value work that contributes to the goal.

- Ensure that the bottleneck works on only one thing at a time. We want to get things done, so stop starting and start finishing.

- Remove any non-throughput producing work from the bottleneck.

- Shield the bottleneck from the interruption and quickly remove impediments, but don't shield them from important information like customer input and feedback.

- Ensure that the bottleneck is never idle or waiting for information, equipment, or material.

1.19.4 Subordinate Decisions to the Bottleneck

Let's look at some key pointers on subordinating decisions to the bottleneck:

- Subordinating decisions means the rest of the system works to help the bottleneck produce the maximum value.

- People other than the bottleneck have some slack. If everyone is working toward the same goal, anyone working beyond the pace of the bottleneck is not increasing the throughput of the system.

- Some approaches you can use are:

  o Ensure that the work, information, and materials received by the bottleneck as input to their work is of highest quality.

  o Have everyone work to the pace of the bottleneck (not faster or slower).

  o Someone else may be able to take some non-specialized tasks from the bottleneck. At this stage, only have someone take on tasks if it doesn't require a large investment in time or money.

1.19.5 Elevate the Bottleneck

Let's look at some key pointers to elevate the bottleneck:

- Elevating the bottleneck requires time and money, so it's done only after exploiting and subordinating.

- You can elevate the bottleneck and improve performance by:

  o Getting more people that can do the same work as the bottleneck.

  o Buying more or faster machines.

o   Giving people training and better tools.

o   Coaching for individual improvement.

o   Improving the workspace.

o   Changing organizational policies.

1.19.6 Manage the Bottleneck

Let's look at some key pointers to manage the bottleneck:

- Manage bottleneck with WIP Limits and Commitment Point

- Consider the impact of the bottleneck's position in the workflow

- Apply WIP limits to smooth outflow relieving the bottleneck

- If WIP limits are quite liberal in bottleneck, and there is a lot of context switching, consider lowering the WIP limit

- If it doesn't have a WIP limit, consider setting one

- Consider the commitment point

This will minimize the negative impact of bottleneck and manipulate bottlenecks to improve the flow. Your description may vary, depending on what part of the principle stands out most for you, but the above-mentioned are possible abbreviations.

Cumulative Flow Diagram Example

Cumulative Flow Diagram (CFD) is defined as a stacked line chart that shows the delivery rate and work-in-progress for multiple states or activities. Let's take an example.

Here's how it works. Every day, count how many items are in each column, and then visualize it in a CFD like this:

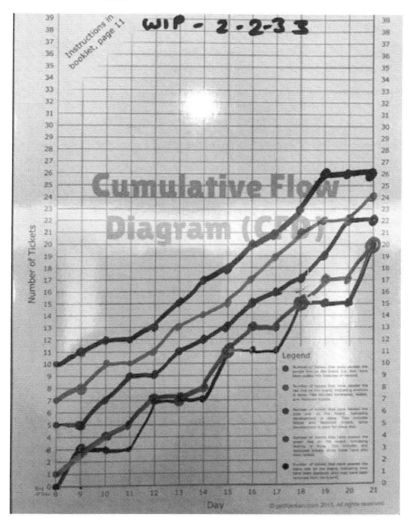

Figure 1.26: Cumulative flow diagram example (Image Source: leankanban.com)

Cumulative flow diagrams seem to be replacing burn down charts for more mature Agile teams and organizations for good reasons. They are easy/easier to update and give you a better insight into the project's status. For those unfamiliar with the concept of CFDs, they simply display the current amount of work in your system for each stage over time. While this may sound simplistic, it provides you with the same kind of information as the traditional burn down chart, plus a lot more. The following figure shows an example of a CFD.

Cumulative Flow Diagram

The Cumulative Flow Diagram (CFD) was introduced by Lean thought leaders, *Don Reinertsen* and *David Anderson*:

- CFD is an important tool for tracking and forecasting Agile projects
- It shows work in different states: Total scope, In-Progress, and Completed
- The report provides an insight into the Burn-up chart, Cycle Time, Work In-Progress, and Bottlenecks in one place
- With this information, the ScrumMaster can focus on the areas requiring attention and improve the team's throughput

The gradient of the "*done*" area describes your velocity over time, while the space between this line and the "*backlog*" line may be defined as WIP. If the width of a part of the WIP area increases, it could indicate that a bottleneck is occurring. If the gradient of the "*backlog*" area is steeper than the gradient of the "done" area, it is a clear sign that you are adding more work to your system than your current capacity. Projecting where the gradients of "*backlog*" and "*done*" will cross is your current best guess of a final release date. The Average Cycle time and Quantity in queue can also be established from the diagram:

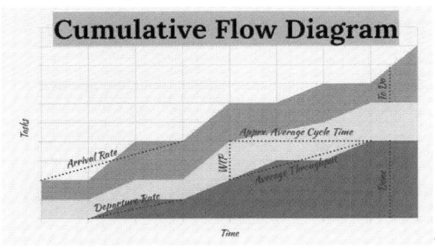

Figure 1.27: *Cumulative flow diagram (Image Source: leankanban.com)*

To compare the arriving requests with the completed work, you can use Cumulative Flow Diagrams (CFDs), which map arrival rate onto closure rate data. CFD helps determine the amount of inventory in the system. Little's law states that at a given WIP level, the ratio of Work In-Progress (WIP) to Cycle Time (CT) equals throughput (T).

KANBAN Board – Handling Bottlenecks

Bottleneck is defined as an activity whose delivery rate constrains the delivery rate achievable from the system as a whole.

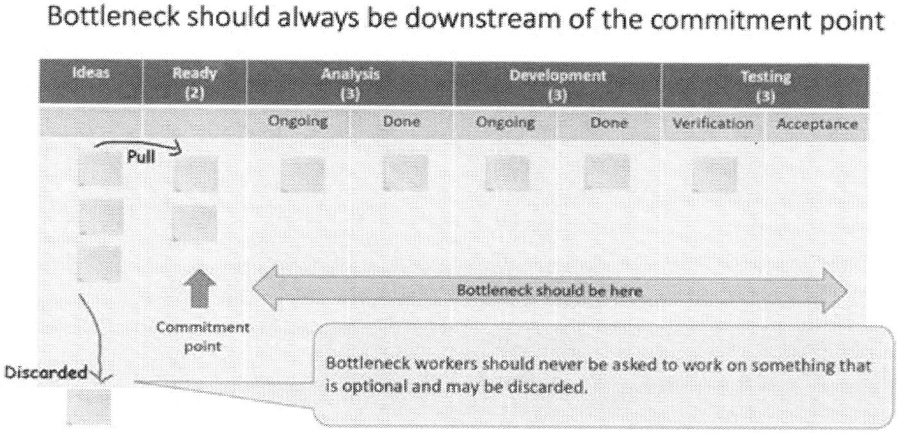

Figure 1.28: KANBAN board – Handling bottlenecks (Image Source: leankanban.com)

Kanban exposes bottlenecks, queues, variability, and waste, all of which impact the performance of the ITSM process via the quantity of valuable work delivered and the cycle time required to deliver it.

1.20 What is Kanban?

The word KANBAN is derived from the combination of two Japanese words: Kan ("*visual*") and ban (card or board), Kanban roughly translates to sign board or signal board. It is a process of manufacturing or work space organization that relies upon visual signals to control inventory. It has become synonymous with Just in Time production (JIT) and demand scheduling.

What is KANBAN?

Kanban

Kanban (看板) (signboard or billboard in Japanese) is a scheduling system for lean manufacturing and just-in-time manufacturing (JIT). Taiichi Ohno, an industrial engineer at Toyota, developed **kanban** to improve manufacturing efficiency.

Figure 1.29: *What is KANBAN (Image Source: leankanban.com)*

KANBAN has its origins from the different tools that TAAICHI Ohno developed at Toyota to operate the production in a systematic framework:

- It is a set of guidelines on how to adapt the existing delivery methodology such that one may, for example, find bottlenecks more accurately and implement change management more easily.
- CAPACITY = WORK + WASTE; COST is not in the ACTIVITY but in the FLOW.

1.21 Kanban General Practices

The following are the "General Practices" of Kanban:

- Visualize (with a Kanban board 看板) - Make invisible work & workflows visible. Understand and focus on your customers' needs and expectations.
- Limit work-in-progress (with Kanban かんばん) - Control & limit WIP limit based on the volume of work items (Incident, SR, CR).
- Manage flow
- Make policies explicit - Manage the work, let people self-organize around it, start working on PULL rather than PUSH, and reduce multi-tasking.
- Implement feedback loops - Evolve your management policies to improve customer & business outcomes, put focus on FIRST TIME RIGHT Quality.
- Improve collaboratively, evolve experimentally - Gain agreement to pursue improvement through evolutionary change (using models & the scientific method).

KANBAN General Practices

Let's depict some key pointers on Kanban general practices.

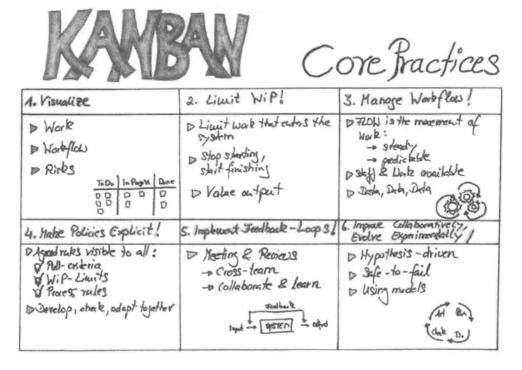

Figure 1.30: KANBAN general practices (Image Source: leankanban.com)

Key principles:

1. **VISIBLE -** Visualize process flow using KANBAN Board
2. **FLOW** – Eliminate waste across the process flow (Waste)
3. **PULL -** Reduce overburdening the resources and avoid multi-tasking (overburdening)
4. **WIP -** Limit the total no of items being worked upon across stages as per capacity and capability (unevenness)
5. **MEASURE -** Defined against purpose to minimize VARIATION

Project reporting tool is used to reflect updated status of the work at the task level; it eases project monitoring and control.

KANBAN Core Practices - Example

Let's depict some examples on Kanban general practices.

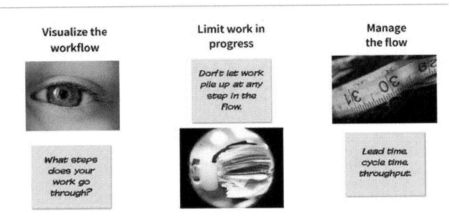

Figure 1.31: KANBAN core practices - Example (Image Source: leankanban.com)

We've said that agile is a mindset and not a specific set of practices, and many agile teams end up tailoring their agile methodology to their own circumstances.

KANBAN Core Practices - Example 2

Let's depict some examples on Kanban core practices:

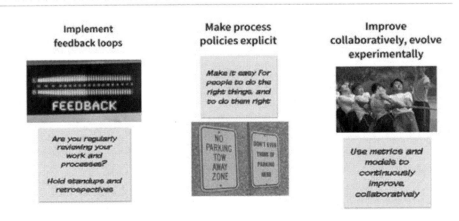

Figure 1.32: KANBAN core practices - Example (Image Source: leankanban.com)

We've said that agile is a mindset and not a specific set of practices, and many agile teams end up tailoring their agile methodology to their own circumstances.

KANBAN Workflow

Limit Work In-Progress (WIP): Control & limit WIP limit based on the volume of Work items (Incident, SR, and CR).

Assign explicit limits to show upper limits how many items may be in progress at each workflow state and highlight when more items exist than the upper limits:

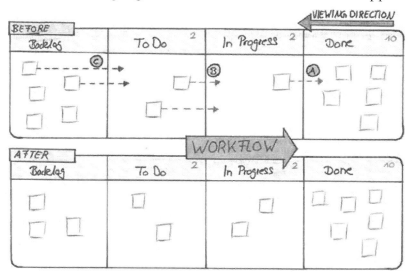

Figure 1.33: KANBAN Workflow (Image Source: leankanban.com)

Start by putting limits on columns in which work is being performed. We've said that agile is a mindset and not a specific set of practices, and many agile teams end up tailoring their agile methodology to their own circumstances.

KANBAN – Limit WIP

Always keep a close eye on the rate of arrival and the rate of departure rate from the system of KANBAN:

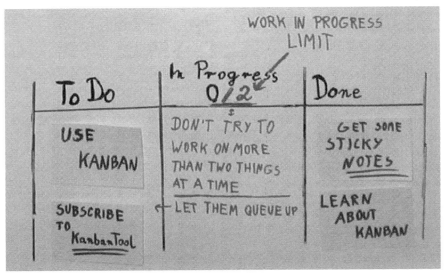

Figure 1.34: KANBAN – Limit WIP (Image Source: leankanban.com)

We've said that agile are a mindset and not a specific set of practices, and many agile teams end up tailoring their agile methodology to their own circumstances. Always keep a close eye on the rate of arrival and the rate of departure rate from the system of KANBAN.

Take a look at your departure/throughput rate. Try to match your arrival rate and departure rate to decide your WIP limit accordingly. If you don't limit your time to market, there is a cost associated with the additional work done, which causes bottlenecks.

Lead Time and Cycle Time

Cycle time is measured from when work starts until it is ready to be delivered, but it may refer to customer lead time, or (very differently) to the reciprocal of delivery rate. Customer lead time is the time that work items take to go through the system— as experienced by the customer. Typically, this is measured from request creation to delivery/the ticket being resolved.

Try to measure your finish date and start date and lead time. Try to see where the maximum delay is occurring in the system and why:

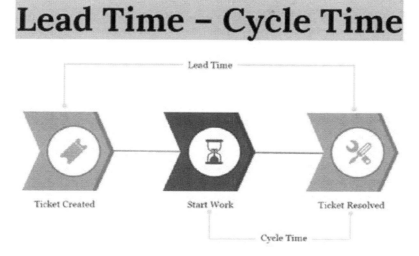

Figure 1.35: Lead time and Cycle time (Image Source: leankanban.com)

We've said that agile are a mindset, not a specific set of practices, and many agile teams end up tailoring their agile methodology for their own circumstances.

Cycle Time Example

Let's depict some example(s) on cycle time:

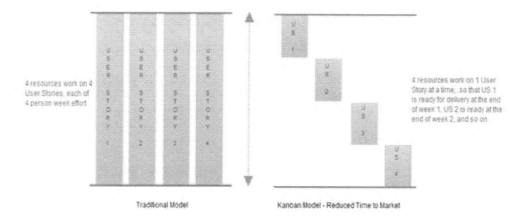

Figure 1.36: Cycle time example (Image Source: leankanban.com)

We've said that agile is a mindset and not a specific set of practices, and many agile teams end up tailoring their agile methodology to their own circumstances.

Cumulative Flow Diagram Instance

Let's depict some instance(s) on cumulative flow diagram. You can use Cumulative Flow Diagrams (CFDs) to compare arriving requests with completed work, which map arrival rate onto closure rate data:

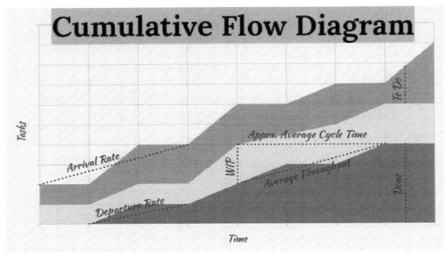

Figure 1.37: Cumulative Flow Diagram instance (Image Source: leankanban.com)

Cumulative Flow Diagram (CFD) is defined as a stacked line chart that shows the delivery rate and work-in-progress for multiple states or activities. We've said that agile is a mindset and not a specific set of practices, and many agile teams end up tailoring their agile methodology to their own circumstances.

1.22 Why Kanban

Time-boxed iterative development has challenges. Common problems include:

- Short time-boxes give more frequent opportunity to measure progress and inspect software but force development items to be smaller. In reality, some items need longer time to finish (ex: problem management in the maintenance phase).
- Smaller development items are often too small to be valuable and difficult to identify.
- The quality of requirements suffers as analysts rush to prepare for the upcoming cycles.

- The quality of current development suffers when busy analysts are unable to inspect software or answer questions during development.
- Quality often suffers as testers race to complete work late in the development time-box.

We've said that agile is a mindset and not a specific set of practices, and many agile teams end up tailoring their agile methodology to their own circumstances.

1.23 Benefits of Kanban

Let's see some key pointers on the benefits of Kanban:

- Transparency
- Relief from overburdening
- Reduced multitasking
- Improved quality
- People engaged emotionally
- More collaboration
- Greater empathy
- Deliver features faster with shorter cycle times
- Responsiveness to change
- Kanban is ideal when priorities change very frequently
- Most customer-centric features are always being worked by effective demand and supply management
- Improve the chances of motivated, empowered, and higher-performing team members by rapid feedback loops
- Requires minimum infrastructure/setup cost, it requires fewer organization/room set-up changes to get started
- Removes activities and reduces waste that doesn't add value to the team/department/organization

Check customer issues and try to deliver customer-centric solutions to suffice customer purpose based on market conditions using KANBAN.

Control WIP limits and remove the ageing bucket of long pending tickets.

Maintain quick response to customer issues.

Reduce the cost of delay, transaction, waste/extra resources etc. as it is another value addition of KANBAN.

Focus on change management process, change control board (CCB), and change advisory board (CAB) to manage the effective inflow and outflow rate of the volume of tickets to our team working in project.

1.24 Ten Things About Kanban

Let's look at some key pointers on Kanban:

- Every Kanban system is unique
- Kanban is about the focus and flow
- Kanban is about evolutionary change, not revolutionary
- Kanban is committed to agility
- Kanban is grounded in reality
- Kanban is a living system
- Kanban is a risk management method
- Kanban balances demand and capacity
- Kanban isn't only for software development or IT
- Kanban works at scale

Check the full organizational ecosystem rather than looking into local optimization while implementing KANBAN.

1.25 Six Forms of Proto Kanban

Proto-KANBAN is a pre-cursor where a visual board exists but a pull system and a service delivery workflow are still emerging. Six forms have been observed:

Aggregated Personal Kanban (in the office)

Single board with rows for each personal KANBAN of each team member

Aggregated Personal Kanban

Let's take a look at some key pointers on personal Kanban:

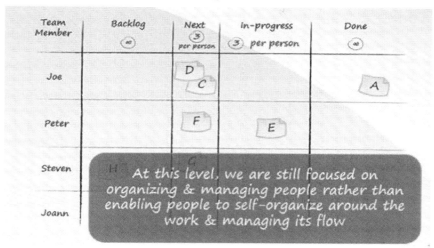

Figure 1.38: Aggregated Personal Kanban (Image Source - leankanban.com)

We've said that agile is a mindset and not a specific set of practices, and many agile teams end up tailoring their agile methodology to their own circumstances.

Team Kanban

Essentially, a personal Kanban board is for a small group of people (usually 3 to 4) who collaborate on the same tasks.

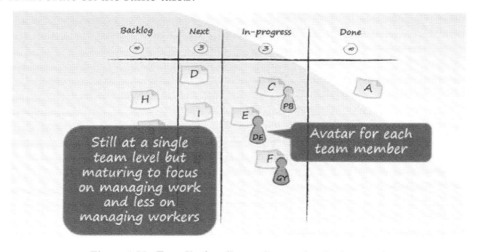

Figure 1.39: Team Kanban (Image Source - leankanban.com)

We've said that agile is a mindset and not a specific set of practices, and many agile teams end up tailoring their agile methodology to their own circumstances.

Emergent Workflow / Portfolio Kanban

Wide column using horizontal positioning to visualize percentage complete.

Simple Portfolio Visualization

Let's look at some key pointers on simple portfolio Kanban:

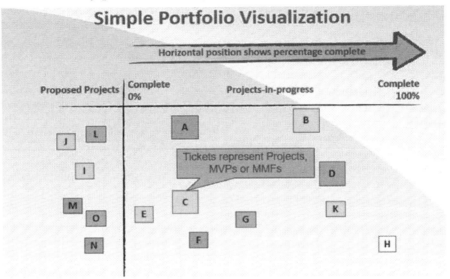

Figure 1.40: *Simple Portfolio Visualization (Image Source - leankanban.com)*

We've said that agile is a mindset and not a specific set of practices, and many agile teams end up tailoring their agile methodology to their own circumstances.

Per person WIP limit

It visualizes some workflow but is not a pull system.

- Often implemented with avatars
- Common with SCRUMBAN hybrids

Per Person WIP Limit

Let's look at some key pointers on per person WIP limit:

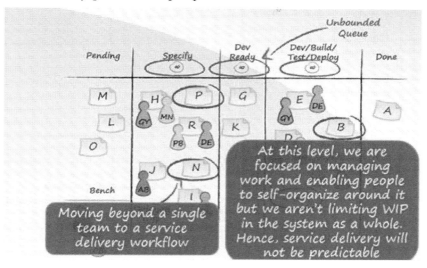

Figure 1.41: Per Person WIP Limit (Image Source - leankanban.com)

We've said that agile is a mindset and not a specific set of practices, and many agile teams end up tailoring their agile methodology to their own circumstances.

Aggregated Team Kanban

Chained To-Do, Doing, Done boards. Again, it displays workflow but still isn't an end-to-end pull system.

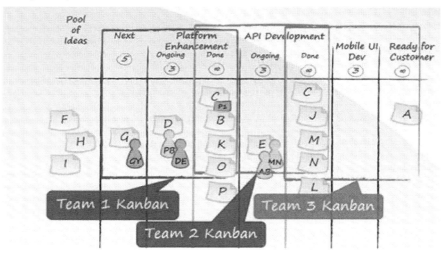

Figure 1.42: Aggregated Team Kanban (Image Source - leankanban.com)

We've said that agile is a mindset and not a specific set of practices, and many agile teams end up tailoring their agile methodology to their own circumstances.

Aggregated Team Kanban - 2

Let's look at some key pointers on Aggregated Team Kanban:

Figure 1.43: Aggregated Team Kanban (Image Source - leankanban.com)

We've said that agile is a mindset and not a specific set of practices, and many agile teams end up tailoring their agile methodology to their own circumstances.

Decoupled Cadences & Constant WIP

Batches without timeboxed commitments. Common with SCRUMBAN hybrids & combined with Per Person WIP Limit.

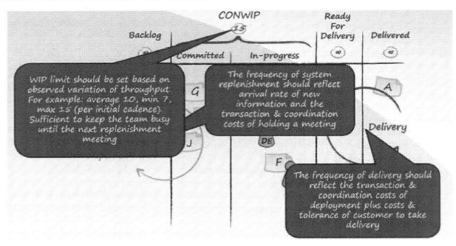

Figure 1.44: Decoupled Cadences & Constant WIP (Image Source - leankanban.com)

We've said that agile is a mindset and not a specific set of practices, and many agile teams end up tailoring their agile methodology to their own circumstances.

1.26 Sample Kanban Board

Is the board up-to-date?

Always keep the dashboard updated. The Kanban dashboard should reflect the correct and updated state of activities at any point of time.

Are you respecting WIP limits?

The team always maintains a smaller number of activity in WIP (6-9 max) for a 5/6 people team. The team concentrates more in getting an activity done faster than doing more activities.

Are you showing blockers and working to remove them?

Always treat blockers with higher priority. Remember that it is interrupting the momentum and eating up your velocity/productivity. Also, daily calls with the stakeholders can be held to remove the blockers, if necessary.

Do you know which task you should be working on and what is next?

Always be aware of the next tasks that clients want to get done. It gives some time to prepare and highlight the concerns upfront. Be updated about your "To-Do" list.

Sample KANBAN board

Let's look at sample example(s) of KANBAN board:

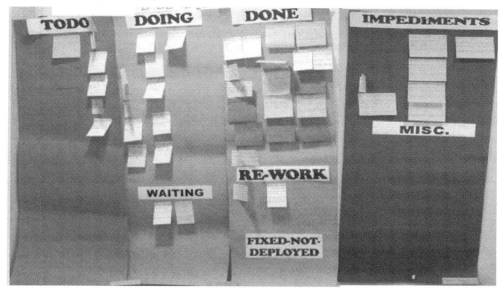

Figure 1.45: *Sample KANBAN Board*

Legend:

- **To Do:** Tickets/Tasks that need to be done. This includes proactive tasks (assigned with no individual)
- **Doing:** Tickets/tasks currently being done by colleague (max three incidents with individual)
- **Done:** Completed tickets/tasks by colleague
- **-Impediments:** Blockers currently

Sample KANBAN board instance

Let's check out sample instance(s) of KANBAN board:

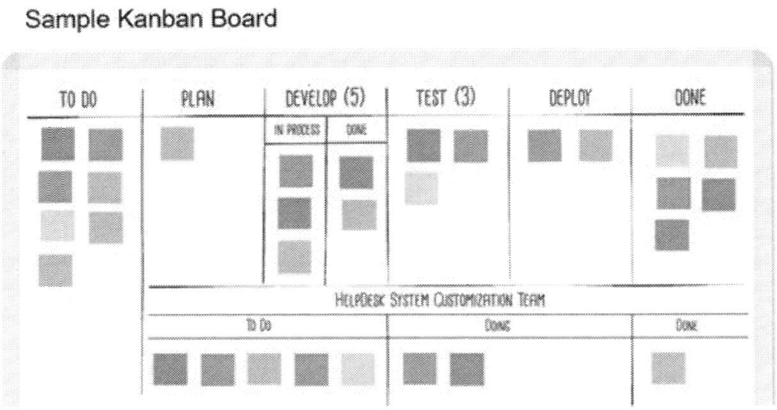

Figure 1.46: Sample KANBAN Board instance (Image Source - leankanban.com)

We've said that agile is a mindset and not a specific set of practices, and many agile teams end up tailoring their agile methodology to their own circumstances:

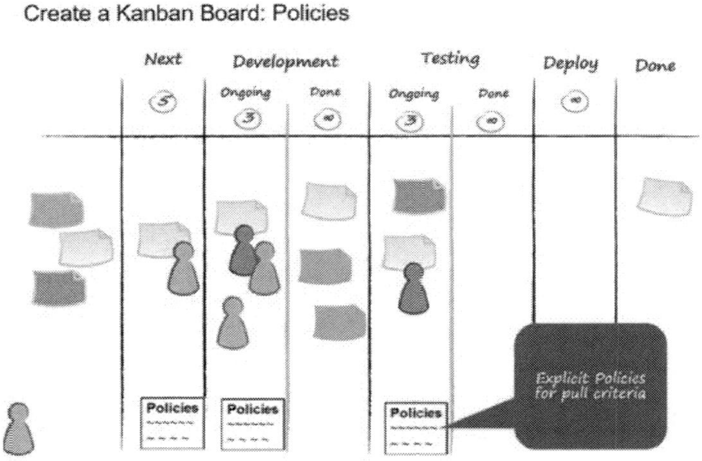

Figure 1.47: KANBAN Board Explicit Policies (Image Source - leankanban.com)

Make the policies explicit - Manage the work, let people self-organize around it, start working on PULL rather than PUSH, and reduce multitasking.

1.27 KANBAN Card Template

Let's depict sample KANBAN card template:

Ticket ID	Bug Type	Severity	Assiginee Intitials
Ticket Summary			
Assigned Date	Closed Date	Respond Time (00:00 H)	Total Effort (00:00 H)

Figure 1.48: KANBAN card template

We've said that agile is a mindset and not a specific set of practices, and many agile teams end up tailoring their agile methodology to their own circumstances.

1.28 Kanban and Incident Categorization - Example

Let's depict an example of KANBAN and incident categorization:

Color Coding	Severity Demarkation in Board	Severity Demarkation In Tool
RED	H+	P1/S1
BLACK	H	P2/S2
BLACK	M	P3/S3
BLACK	L	P4/S4

Figure 1.49: Kanban and incident categorization - Example

Legend - P --> Priority, S --> Severity

Priority Marked with – H+/ H / M / L

Color coding:

- All the sticky should be light yellow
- All the text in the sticky should be black

The highest priority ticket should me marked in RED as H.

1.29 JIRA Ticket/User Profile

User profile:

- Group-ID for team
- Individual JIRA ID for each member

User Profile
JIRA id
Full Name
email-id
TimeZone : JIRA Default
Groups : Based on account

Figure 1.50: JIRA user profile

We've said that agile is a mindset and not a specific set of practices, and many agile teams end up tailoring their agile methodology to their own circumstances.

Ticket profile:

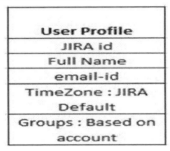

Ticket Category
Bug
Task
New Feature
Proactive Maintenance
Production Support

Sevirity
Sev1
Sev2+
Sev2
Sev3+
Sev3
Sev4

Ticket Status
In Progress
Reopened
Resolved
Validated
More Info Required
Not Reproducible
Confirmed
AMS Analysis
AMS confirmed

Ticket Resolution
Open
Resolved
Unresolved
Closed
Onhold
Fixed
Fixed Not Deployed
Duplicate

Figure 1.51: Ticket profile

We've said that agile is a mindset and not a specific set of practices, and many agile teams end up tailoring their agile methodology to their own circumstances.

1.30 JIRA Tool Best Practice – Dashboard

Let's illustrate some JIRA tool best practice(s):

Issue Statistics: LHPROD IBM Bugs (Priority)

Priority	Count	Percentage	
↑ Sev 2	7		9%
↓ Sev 3+	10		12%
↓ Sev 3	56		68%
↓ Sev 4	9		11%
Total	82		

Issue Statistics: LHPROD IBM Tasks (Priority)

Priority	Count	Percentage	
↓ Sev 3	7		100%
Total	7		

Issue Statistics: LHPROD IBM Features (Priority)

Priority	Count	Percentage	
↑ Sev 2	1		25%
↓ Sev 3+	1		25%
↓ Sev 3	2		50%
Total	4		

Figure 1.52: JIRA tool issue statistics dashboard

We've said that agile is a mindset and not a specific set of practices, and many agile teams end up tailoring their agile methodology to their own circumstances.

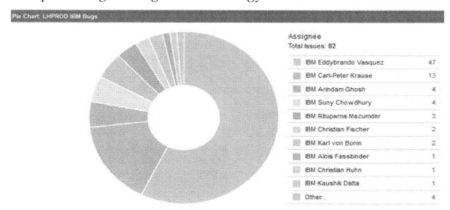

Pie Chart: LHPROD IBM Bugs

Assignee
Total Issues: 82

Assignee	Count
IBM Eddybrando Vasquez	47
IBM Carl-Peter Krause	13
IBM Arindam Ghosh	4
IBM Suny Chowdhury	4
IBM Rituparna Mazumder	3
IBM Christian Fischer	2
IBM Karl von Bonin	2
IBM Alois Fassbinder	1
IBM Christian Huhn	1
IBM Kaushik Datta	1
Other	4

Figure 1.53: JIRA tool assignee statistics dashboard

We've said that agile is a mindset and not a specific set of practices, and many agile teams end up tailoring their agile methodology to their own circumstances.

1.31 Kanban - Critical & Emergency Events

Let's depict some KANBAN critical and emergency event(s). Here's a KANBAN – emergency & business critical events instance:

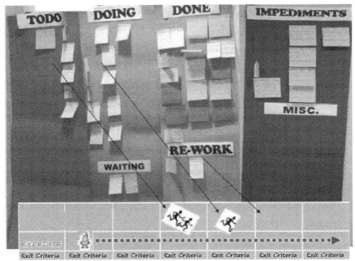

Figure 1.54: KANBAN – Emergency & Business critical events

We've said that agile is a mindset and not a specific set of practices, and many agile teams end up tailoring their agile methodology to their own circumstances.

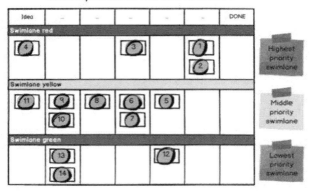

Figure 1.55: KANBAN Board – Different Swimlane (Image Source - leankanban.com)

We've said that agile is a mindset and not a specific set of practices, and many agile teams end up tailoring their agile methodology to their own circumstances.

1.32 Enabling Agile Ways of Working Across the Organization

Organizations are a collection of employees, contractors, suppliers, and customers as well as the wider stakeholder community. All of these groups interact to define, plan, enable, co-create, and deliver value.

The complex aspects of an organization, including its people, activities, tools, and processes, all connect in nuanced, interdependent ways. The introduction of an agile way of working in one part of the organization, while potentially proving locally effective, is unlikely to accrue organizational benefit.

> **Key message**
>
> **The whole organization needs to develop agility for the co-created value to be fully optimized.**

If this whole organization approach to agility is not followed, a team that has embraced agile ways of working may ultimately be hindered by other teams, internal and external, that have not adapted similarly. The team may even need to revert to its previous ways of working to deliver results.

We already explained the relationships between various parts of an organization and looked at an example of the impact of one team or department changing its practices.

"If this whole organization approach to agility is not followed, an agile team may ultimately be hindered by other teams".

1. **The team:** This can be any part of the organization that delivers service(s) or product(s) to a customer or to another team within the organization. This will be described later as the Agile SHIFT team, but we will simply call them 'the team' for now. The team has been positioned in the centre of this diagram to easily demonstrate that it is interacting with every other element of the organization, affecting and being affected by them.

2. **Who supports the team?:** Traditionally, several organizational functions are referred to as support functions. However, we need to take a wider view and consider that there is a sense of mutual support across the organization.

3. **Using HR as an example:** To illustrate the concepts, imagine that the HR department has made a decision to change the way in which it records resource usage across the entire organization in order to deliver benefits and

value in efficiency and effectiveness. HR now sits in the centre, becoming, for this example, the team.

4. **Mutual support:** For the HR initiative to be successful, every other part of the organization will need to change some of their ways of working, as success is totally dependent on their response.

5. **External stakeholders:** Successful organizations will generally consider external suppliers and stakeholders as an integral part of their ecosystem. They play an important role in the co-creation of value, so it is important that they are seen as part of the wider organization, understanding and responding to the changes being made.

6. **Organizational alignment:** This is an important strategic goal. It is essential that different initiatives become aligned and move in the same direction.

Relationships between various parts of an organization – instance:

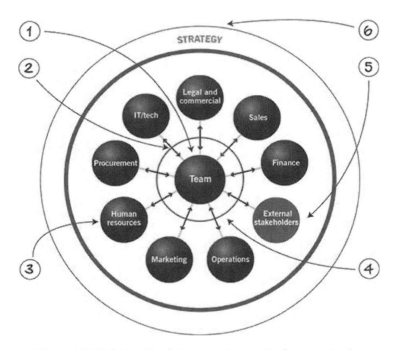

Figure 1.56: Relationships between various parts of an organization
(Image source: https://www.axelos.com)

We've said that agile is a mindset and not a specific set of practices, and many agile teams end up tailoring their agile methodology to their own circumstances.

1.33 The Agile SHIFT Framework

This guidance has explained the rationale behind Agile SHIFT. It considered the changing context in which most organizations find themselves. This has come about because of:

- VUCA (Volatility, Uncertainty, Complexity, and Ambiguity)
- Technology
- Disruptors
- Deltas

The response to this is to seek enterprise agility, and this is what Agile SHIFT presents as the solution to the changing context.

The dangers of separating change and innovation from the mainstream activities of running the organization were discussed. It was stressed that RTO and CTO must co-exist in a symbiotic relationship. Multimodal working was recommended as a way of having several responses that can be deemed appropriate.

Lastly, we considered the organization-wide perspective of transformation. Organizations are a network of interconnecting and interdependent entities, all of which must work in unison for the organization to succeed in its aims and objectives.

Key message

The focus of Agile SHIFT is to help create a culture of enterprise agility across the entire organization, with a particular emphasis on front-line and back-office support teams who are often on the receiving end of transformational initiatives.

Some transformations are enterprise-scaled, and these should be led and managed by transformation management professionals, such as program managers, who are experienced in the art of moving people and organizations forward. However, every individual in the organization is responsible for both RTO and CTO, which makes them co-creators of value. For this to be achieved successfully, teams need to work in more agile ways.

Having considered why we need Agile SHIFT, we must now focus on the 'what' and the 'how,' as illustrated in *Figure 1.57*. The Agile SHIFT framework comprises the following elements:

- **An enablement of agile ways of working:** All parts of the enterprise must be in strategic alignment to ensure successful transformation.

- **Agile SHIFT principles:** A set of fundamental rules that guide an organization in all circumstances.

- **Agile SHIFT practices:** A set of practical approaches that will bring real benefits to any team wishing to work in more agile ways.

- "Every individual in the organization is responsible for both RTO and CTO, which makes them co-creators of value."

  The Agile SHIFT delivery approach: This approach encompasses three key roles: the Agile SHIFT team, the Agile SHIFT coach, and the Agile SHIFT sponsor, and how a team can perform more effectively.

- **The Agile SHIFT workflow:** A cycle of iterative steps where the team works in short bursts, followed by feedback and decision making.

- **An Agile SHIFT iteration:** A detailed look at the activities within an iteration.

- **Tools and techniques:** These can be used as appropriate to help in any Agile SHIFT initiative.

- Agile SHIFT framework – instance:

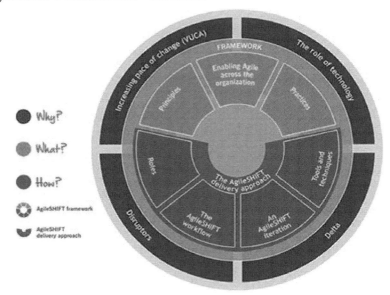

Figure 1.57: Agile SHIFT framework (Image source: https://www.axelos.com)

We've said that agile is a mindset and not a specific set of practices, and many agile teams end up tailoring their agile methodology to their own circumstances.

1.34 Dynamic Systems Development Method

The Dynamic Systems Development Method (DSDM) was developed in the 1990s to provide more discipline to Rapid Application Development (RAD), and the latest version is called Atern.

The following are the features of DSDM:

- It uses a prioritization technique called MoSCoW (Must, Should, Could, and Won't) to determine the requirements to be included in a release or iteration.

- The Atern methodology fixes the schedule, cost, and quality.

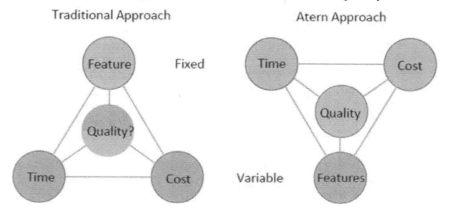

Figure 1.58: Dynamic Systems Development Method (Image source: https://www.scrumalliance.com)

The following are the eight DSDM Atern principles:

- **Principle 1 - Focus on the business need**

   Every project decision should be viewed in the light of the overriding project goal, which is to deliver what the business needs, when it needs it.

   So, it is important to understand the true business priorities and develop a sound business case, while seeking continuous business sponsorship and commitment and be able to guarantee the Minimum Usable Subset (MUS – explained later).

- **Principle 2 – Deliver on time**

   This is met using Timeboxes while focusing on the business priorities so that deadlines are always met. It uses the MoSCoW approach to prioritization.

- **Principle 3 – Collaborate**

   Teams that collaborate gain increased understanding, greater speed, and shared ownership, all done in a spirit of cooperation and commitment. Such teams or groups will always achieve higher performance than those that are more loosely associated.

   To help make this principle, Atern teams involve the right stakeholders at the right time, ensuring that the teams are empowered, and they actively involve the business representatives.

- **Principle 4 – Never compromise quality**

  The level of quality that the project needs to deliver should be agreed at the start. This solution has to be 'good enough,' and as long as the features contained within the minimum usable subset have been delivered, the solution should be deemed acceptable.

  The level of quality is built in by constant and regular reviews, with a philosophy of 'test early and continuously'.

- **Principle 5 – Build incrementally from firm foundations**

  Atern advocates incremental delivery in order to deliver real business benefits early, resulting in an increase of stakeholder confidence in addition to providing a useful source of feedback for subsequent increments. Atern advocates the style of Enough Design-Up-Front (EDUF) by understanding the scope of a business problem in an outline form but not so detailed that the project becomes paralyzed.

  This is supported by continual confirmation that the correct solution is being built, which is done by checking the project's ongoing viability and reassessing priorities as and when needed.

- **Principle 6 – Develop iteratively**

  This allows the project to converge on an accurate business solution, as it is very rare for any product to be built perfectly the first time. For this reason, a pragmatic and informal approach is taken to change control, which, in turn, relies on iteration and produces a better solution.

  By accepting the fact that most detail emerges later, change can be embraced by being creative, experimenting, learning, and evolving. Since change is inevitable, Atern allows for change and harnesses its benefits.

- **Principle 7 – Communicate continuously and clearly**

  Atern techniques are designed to improve communication receptiveness since poor project communication is often cited as the biggest cause of project failure. Atern teams run daily standup meetings, use facilitated workshops, and keep documentation lean and timely while encouraging informal face-to-face communication.

- **Principle 8 – Demonstrate control**

  Atern teams, especially the project manager, will use an appropriate level of formality when tracking, reporting, and making plans and progress visible to everyone. Progress is measured on the delivery of products rather than activities, and the project viability is continually evaluated based on the business objectives. Control is done 'bottom-up' by ensuring that the solution development time box level has a fixed end date, and this helps keep the increment level time boxes on track, as a result of which the project time box level will also deliver on time.

Well-defined time boxes with constant review points and associated plans help follow this principle.

Phases of DSDM

The following are the phases of DSDM:

- **Pre-project:** Identify the right project for delivering business value
- **Feasibility:** Identify the most feasible solution for the project
- **Foundation:** Establish a strong-foundation for the project on the business and technical fronts
- **Exploration:** Iteratively and incrementally develop the solution that is not expected to be ready
- **Engineering:** Iteratively and incrementally develop non-functional requirements
- **Post-project:** Assess the business benefits realized through solution delivery
- **Deployment:** Deploy the solution to production/the end user.

1.35 The New Role of the Manager

Let's see some key pointers on the role of the manager. The following table can help understand the type of mindset shift expected from different stakeholders:

Traditional manger	Agile coach/new role of manager
Decide and assign tasks to the team consultants	Groom team members and provide coaching
Carry out status review of work progress of team members	Protect team members from unnecessary disruptions and guide them to right direction Keep track of how much work is pending
Give delivery/milestone deadlines on behalf of team members	Provide input on features, functionality, and other aspects of what's being produced
Direct the team on how to work so that they can meet the commitment	Carry out performance evaluations and provide feedback to team members
Convince the team that the commitments made on their behalf are attainable	Provide advice and input to the team on difficult technical issues that come up

Monitor the team's progress to ensure that they stay on schedule and aren't facing problems	Plan training for team and carry out career-development and planning with team members
Conduct weekly updates and 1:1 meeting with team to identify issues and provide direction	Stay abreast of the latest developments in the technology that the team uses, industry news, etc.
Recruit, interview, and hire new members in the team	Plan and oversee budgets and financials, and think about tools, skills, and other future needs
Fire team members who are consistently unable to perform	Help remove impediments that the team is unable or not well-placed to resolve themselves

Table 1.6: The new role of the manager

Your description may vary, depending on what part of the principle stands out most for you, but the above-mentioned are possible abbreviations.

Leading effectively:

The key element of building Agility is a mindset. The next table can help understand the type of mindset shift expected from different stakeholders:

Management focus	Leadership focus
Tasks/things	People
Control	Empowerment
Efficiency	Effectiveness
Doing things right	Doing the right things
Speed	Direction
Practices	Principles
Command	Communication

Table 1.7: Leading effectively

Servant leadership:

- Shield team from interruptions
- Remove impediments to progress
- Re(communicate) project vision
- Carry food and water

Leadership tools and techniques:

- Modeling desired behavior – Honesty, forward-looking, competent, inspiring
- Communicating the project vision

- Enabling others to act
- Being willing to challenge the status quo

Your description may vary, depending on what part of the principle stands out most for you, but the above-mentioned are possible abbreviations.

1.36 Kanban vs. SCRUM

Let's discuss some key pointers on the differences of Kanban vs. Scrum:

KANBAN	SCRUM
No prescribed roles	Scrum prescribes roles like scrum master, product owner, and team member
Work is 'pulled' through the system (single piece flow)	Work is 'pulled' through the system in batches (the sprint backlog)
Measured by cycle time	Measured by velocity
Continuous delivery	Time boxed delivery
Changes can be made at any time	No changes allowed mid-sprint
More appropriate in operational environments with a high degree of variability in priority; here, the volume of work is unpredictable, and the team is generally mature	More appropriate in situations where work can be prioritized in batches that can be left alone; here, the volume of work is predictable, and the team can be new

Table 1.8: Kanban Vs. Scrum

Your description may vary, depending on what part of the principle stands out most for you, but the above-mentioned are possible abbreviations.

1.37 Conclusion

In this chapter, we mainly explored the following:

- Agile SCRUM KANBAN XP DSDM Lean etc. values, principles, different types, general practices, & best practices adoption
- Management focus vs. leadership focus
- KANBAN Vs. SCRUM
- Waterfall Vs. Agile
- Agile estimation and planning at portfolio level
- Agile contracts field rules for better results and faster performance

- Backlog management in Agile

- Agile framework

- How Agile mapped to traditional practices

- Understand critical success factors of adopting Agile over the Waterfall model

- Managing bottlenecks with KANBAN

- Agile evolved in the late 1990s in response to the burdens of heavy documentation and frequent changes in requirements

- The Agile Manifesto was signed by 17 software developers in 2001, and it captured the values and principles of the Agile movement

- The Agile Manifesto highlights 12 principles

- As a lightweight project management approach, Agile avoids big design, heavy documentation, and top-down management or control

- Agile emphasizes collaboration, team empowerment, and frequent demonstrations of progress by focusing on Pull vs. Push

- Agile increases return on investment by focusing on continuous flow of value

- Agile delivers reliable results by engaging customers in frequent interactions and shared ownership

- Agile expects uncertainty and manages it through iterations, anticipation, and adaptation

- Agile unleashes creativity and innovation by recognizing that individuals are the ultimate source of value and creating an environment where they can make a difference

- Agile boosts performance through group accountability for results and shared responsibility for team effectiveness

- Agile improves effectiveness and reliability through situation-specific strategies, processes, and practices

  The ccrum masters, product owners, developers, and professionals closely associated with Agile Scrum, Kanban, and XP projects can further improve their knowledge of Agile with valuable pragmatic insights. Entry-level professionals and Agile enthusiasts with relevant experience can also acquire in-depth knowledge of the concepts discussed in the Agile methodology tutorial.

- Advocate for agile principles and values to create a shared mindset

- Ensure a common understanding of agile
- Support change through educating and influencing
- Practice transparency in order to enhance trust
- Create a safe environment for experimentation
- Experiment with new techniques and processes
- Share knowledge through collaboration
- Encourage emergent leadership via a safe environment
- Practice servant leadership

Here's another way of summing up the core principles of agile.

- Welcoming change
- Working in small, value-added increments
- Using build and feedback loops
- Learning through discovery
- Value-driven development
- Failing fast with learning
- Continuous delivery
- Continuous improvement

In the next chapter, you should be able to:

- Understand numerous lessons learnt and take a pragmatic approach to help sustain customer relationships and enhance business/Customer delights
- Understand the tricky tips & traps of Agile, Scrum, KANBAN, etc.

We've said that agile is a mindset and not a specific set of practices, and many agile teams end up tailoring their agile methodology to their own circumstances.

Let's take up some review questions.

1.38 Questions

1. **In "Full project lifecycle," DSDM Atern is an approach derived from project management and product delivery _____.**

    Select the correct answer(s).

    a. Mandatory standards

    b. Formal consensus

    c.   Best practices

    d.   Dynamic methodologies

    e.   Informal consensus

2. **In "Full project lifecycle," DSDM Atern philosophy and the set of principles are supported by the four pillars of:**
   Select the correct answer(s).
       a.   Practices, products, process, and people

       b.   Practices, processes, themes, and activities

       c.   Timeboxes, foundations, products, and planning

       d.   Planning, foundations, products, and activities

       e.   Practices, planning, foundations, and themes

3. **In "Full project lifecycle," DSDM Atern places strong emphasis on delivering solutions that:**
   Select the correct answer(s).
       a.   Provide detailed plans

       b.   Are derived from technical design

       c.   Satisfy the real requirements of business

       d.   Are derived from initial baseline functionality

       e.   Are derived from non-functional requirements

4. **In "Full project lifecycle," the DSDM Atern principle of "Focus on the business need" means Atern teams will:**
   Select the correct answer(s).
       a.   Build a one-team culture

       b.   Test early and continuously

       c.   Manage proactively

       d.   Apply the 80:20 rule

       e.   Establish a sound business case

5. **In "Full project lifecycle," the DSDM Atern principle of "Demonstrate control" means that the Atern project manager and the team leader will:**
   Select the correct answer(s).
       a.   Use an appropriate level_of_formality

       b.   Use facilitated workshops

       c.   Converge on an accurate solution

    d.   Establish an understanding of what the business is

    e.   Make PLANS AND PROGRESS visible to all.

6.   **In "Full project lifecycle," the DSDM Atern principle of "Deliver on time" means the Atern Teams will:**

   Select the correct answer(s).

    a.   Actively engage the business representative(s)

    b.   Focus on business priorities

    c.   Build in quality by constant review

    d.   Do adequate design upfront to create strong foundations

    e.   Always meet deadlines

7.   **In "Full project lifecycle," the DSDM Atern principle of "Communicate continuously and clearly" means the Atern Teams will:**

   Select the correct answer(s).

    a.   Use facilitated workshops

    b.   Manage proactively

    c.   Build a one-team culture

    d.   Continually confirm that a correct solution is being built

    e.   Run daily team stand-up sessions

8.   **When considering DSDM Atern in "Full project lifecycle" based on flexible requirements, what do they mean by 'requirements'?**

   Select the correct answer(s).

   1)   Functionality

   2)   Feature

   3)   Scope

   4)   Design

        a.   2 and 4 only

        b.   1, 2, and 4

        c.   1,2,3, and 4

        d.   1, 2, and 3

        e.   1 and 3 only

9. **Which of following parameters are deemed variable on a DSDM Atern project "Full project lifecycle"?**

   Select the correct answer(s).

   a. Quality

   b. Time

   c. Features

   d. Cost

   e. Quality and time

10. **In "Full project lifecycle," what does DSDM Atern call the most effective way to communicate?**

    Select the correct answer(s).

    a. Structured communication

    b. Separate channel communication

    c. Rich communication

    d. Informal communication

    e. Face-to-face communication using daily team stand-up sessions or facilitated workshops

Question Number	Answer	Explanation
1	c	**Correct Answer(s):** c. In "Full project lifecycle," DSDM Atern is an approach derived from project management and product delivery best practices.
2	a	**Correct Answer(s):** a. In "Full project lifecycle," DSDM Atern philosophy and the set of principles are supported by the four pillars of "Practices, Products, Process and People".
3	c	**Correct Answer(s):** c. In "Full project lifecycle," DSDM Atern places strong emphasis on delivering solutions that satisfy the real requirements of business.
4	d, e	**Correct Answer(s):** d, e. In "Full project lifecycle," the DSDM Atern principle of "Focus on the business need" means Atern teams will - apply the 80:20 rule - establish a sound business case

5	a, e	**Correct Answer(s):** a, e. In "Full project lifecycle," the DSDM Atern principle of "Demonstrate control" means the Atern project manager and the team leader will - use an appropriate LEVEL OF FORMALITY - make PLANS AND PROGRESS visible to all.
6	b, e	**Correct Answer(s):** b, e. In "Full project lifecycle," the DSDM Atern principle of "Deliver on time" means the Atern Teams will - focus on business priorities - always meet deadlines
7	a, e	**Correct Answer(s):** a, e. In "Full project lifecycle", DSDM Atern principle of "Communicate continuously and clearly" means the Atern teams will - use facilitated workshops - run daily team stand-up sessions
8	d	**Correct Answer(s):** d. When considering DSDM Atern in "Full project lifecycle" based on flexing requirements, requirements mean: - Functionality - Feature - Scope
9	c	**Correct Answer(s):** c. Features are deemed variable on a DSDM Atern project "Full project lifecycle."
10	c, e	**Correct Answer(s):** c, e. In "Full project lifecycle," DSDM Atern calls the following ways the most effective way to communicate: - Rich communication - Face-to-face communication using daily team stand-up sessions or facilitated workshops

CHAPTER 2
Lessons Learnt and Pragmatic Approach – Agile Scrum Kanban

Introduction

In this chapter, we will mainly discuss the following topics. After completing this lesson, you will be able to describe/explain/implement:

- The key secrets of Agile leadership
- Categorization of organizational risks
- Address risks with spikes
- FIT FOR PURPOSE – Kanban/Scrum
- Hybrid agile
- Enterprise agility
- Examples of value stream mapping in sales on proposals
- Agile and deepawali celebrations
- PUSH and PULL implementations of Agile methods
- Agile impacts on QA managers
- Different types of dysfunctions in Agile
- Practice transparency through visualization
- Create a safe environment for experimentation
- Experiment with new techniques and processes

- Share knowledge through collaboration
- Encourage emergent leadership via a safe environment
- Lessons learnt and pragmatic approach to help sustain customer relationships and enhance business/customer delights
- Tricky tips & traps on Agile, Scrum, KANBAN, etc

Do you ever worry about not following the lessons learnt, the pragmatic approaches of Agile, Scrum, KANBAN, XP etc., and best practices in your organization(s)/project(s)? Or you/your team are always happy in learning only the theoretical aspects of Agile, Scrum, KANBAN, XP, etc.?

This chapter will help you:

- Understand numerous lessons learnt and pragmatic approach to help sustain customer relationships and enhance business/customer delights
- Understand the tricky tips & traps on Agile, Scrum, KANBAN etc.

We've said that agile is a mindset and not a specific set of practices, and many agile teams end up tailoring their agile methodology to their own circumstances.

Structure

In this chapter, we will discuss the following topics:

- Key secrets of Agile leadership
- Key questions of personal agility
- Categorizing organizational risk
- 7 forces preventing getting to "pull"
- Kanban coaching guidance on "where to start" within large organizations
- Define Muri, Mura, and Muda
- Order to eliminate Muri, Mura, and Muda
- How to achieve elimination of Muri, Mura, and Muda
- Draw "the fit-for-purpose framework"
- Kanban - daily mantra for faster performance and better results
- "Iterative" Vs. "Incremental" Vs. "Agile"
- "Blended" Vs. "Hybrid"
- "Hybrid Agile"
- When should we use hybrid approaches?
- Lessons learnt from Agile leadership team journey
- What's the point of a story point? - story points and their interpretation

- o   Stakeholders' perceptions
- Kanban or scrum? – the best fit for your organization
  - o   What is Scrum?
  - o   What is Kanban?
  - o   Kanban versus Scrum: A thoughtful comparison
  - o   Project recommendations
  - o   Setting up of the architectural runway
  - o   Clarifying the product roadmap
  - o   Creating and testing a working prototype
  - o   Scrum implementation
  - o   Kanban implementation
- Kanban push and pull implementations of Agile methods
- Agile impacts on QA managers
- Recognizing the five symptoms of a poor backlog - a two-part solution
  - o   Understanding the backlog
  - o   Five symptoms of a poor backlog
  - o   Effects of a poor backlog
  - o   Applying a two-part solution
- What Agile can and cannot do - A journey worth understanding
  - o   Scheduling
  - o   Prioritizing
  - o   Reducing costs
  - o   Tracking progress
  - o   Ensuring team satisfaction
- Managing releases in a scrum framework
  - o   Ways to successfully deliver production-deployable code
- Agile and Deepawali celebrations - implementing Kanban unconsciously
- Address risk with spikes
  - o   What is a spike?
  - o   What causes an epic or story to form a spike?
  - o   Guidelines for spikes
- Benefits and barriers to enterprise Agility
- Multimodal working
- Enterprise agility and the creation of smaller-scale agility

- Five dysfunctions of a team
- Top 3 improvement practices of agile
- Example of value stream mapping in sales on proposals

Objectives

After studying this unit, you should be able to:

- Understand numerous lessons learnt and pragmatic approach to help sustain customer relationships and enhance business/customer delights
- Understand the tricky tips & traps on Agile, Scrum, KANBAN, etc.

Let's start.

2.1 Key Secrets of Agile Leadership

Here are some key pointers on the key secrets of Agile leadership:

- Change is easy if you want to do it
- Create clarity on what really matters
- Apply Agility to leadership

2.2 Key Questions of Personal Agility

Let's look at some key pointers on the key secrets of agile leadership. The following are the 6 questions of personal Agility:

- What really matters?
- What did I do last week?
- What could I do this week?
- What is important or urgent?
- What do I want to get done?
- Who can help?

We've said that agile is a mindset and not a specific set of practices, and many agile teams end up tailoring their agile methodology to their own circumstances.

2.3 Categorizing Organizational Risk

Let's look at some key pointers on categorizing organizational risk:

- **Fragile:** At risk of total failure/financial ruin

- **Resilient:** Takes damage, avoids total failure, and recovers; it reflects the capability to bounce back
- **Robust:** Absorbs uncertainty, repels blows, and avoids damage
- **Antifragile:** Responds to stress by mutating and maintains fitness for purpose

Purpose and identity can change entirely.

2.4 Seven Forces Preventing Getting to "pull"

Let's look at some key pointers on the seven forces preventing getting to "pull":

- Not starting with a customer-facing service
- "We are just order takers"
- Legacy tooling unsuitable for evolutionary change
- A lack of understanding of the business risks
- A lack of mathematical literacy; people are busy multi-tasking rather than focusing on finishing than doing
- A lack of skills in negotiation or forming business agreements
- A lack of confidence planning & scheduling at scale

2.5 Kanban Coaching Guidance on "Where to Start" Within Large Organizations

Let's look at some key pointers on the Kanban coaching guidance:

- Must be customer-facing
- Must not be mission critical
- Must be highly visible
- Staff are enthusiastic, indeed may volunteer to pilot the changes

Try to measure your finish date and start date and lead time. Try to see where the maximum delay is occurring in the system and why. Culture follows values, and practices follow culture. Values must always lead; they are something people think help them become transparent.

2.6 Define Muri, Mura, and Muda

Let's see what Muri, Mura, and Muda signify?

- Muri (overburdening)
- Mura (unevenness)
- Muda (waste/non -value adding in the process)

2.7 Order to Eliminate Muri, Mura, and Muda

Let's take a look at the order to eliminate Muri, Mura, and Muda. Eliminate in this order:

1. Muri
2. Mura
3. Muda

2.8 How to Achieve Elimination of Muri, Mura, and Muda?

Let's understand how to achieve elimination of Muri, Mura, and Muda. To have less overburdening, achieve:

- Greater individual pride in their work
- Focus on important jobs

Evenness of flow:

- Greater predictability and customer satisfaction
- Better sense of purpose and mastery

Better economic results:

The Toyota production system, and later, the concept of lean, was developed around eliminating the three types of deviations that show inefficient allocation of resources. The three types are Muda (無駄, waste), Mura (斑, unevenness), and Muri (無理, overburden).

MUDA, waste, can be defined in eight types: 7 defined by Toyota and 'non utilized skills. These are: defects, overproduction, waiting, non-used talent, transport, inventories, motion, and excess processing.

2.9 Draw "The Fit-for-Purpose Framework"

A fit-for-purpose organization continually satisfies its customers with products and services designed, implemented, and delivered in a sustainable manner. The following diagram is the fit-for-purpose framework:

Figure 2.1: *"The fit-for-purpose framework" (Image Source - leankanban.com)*

A fit-for-purpose organization continually satisfies its customers with products and services designed, implemented and delivered in a sustainable manner.

The F4P framework includes guidance on segmenting your market by customer purpose, determining the criteria that customers use to make a selection among competitors, and a powerful call for action on metrics and KPIs.

The F4P framework combines both narrative- and data-based approaches to sensing customer segments and their criteria and assessing fitness. Your company can use these to serve their customers better and to find the right customers to serve.

Understanding the market segments defined by purpose and understanding customers' fitness criteria should be among your business's core strategic capabilities to ensure organizational alignment and long-term survivability of the business.

Please visit **http://www.fitterforpurpose.com** for details.

2.10 Kanban - Daily Mantra for Faster Performance and Better Results

Is the board up-to-date?

Always keep the dashboard updated. In Kanban, the dashboard should reflect the correct and updated state of activities at any point of time.

Are you respecting WIP limits?

The team always maintains a smaller number of activity in WIP (3-4 max) for a 5/6 people team. The team concentrates on getting an activity done faster rather than doing more activities.

Are you showing blockers and working to remove them?

Always treat blockers with higher priority. Remember that they are interrupting the momentum and eating up your velocity. Daily calls can be scheduled with the stakeholders to remove the blockers, if necessary.

Do you know which task you should be working on and what is next?

Always be aware of the next tasks that clients want to get done. It gives you time to prepare and highlight the concerns upfront. Be updated about your "To-Do" list.

2.11 "Iterative" vs. "Incremental" vs. "Agile"

Project lifecycles live on a continuum, ranging from plan-driven on one end to Agile on the other. To help understand this continuum, let's say two of the key aspects of Agility are "deliver early and often" and "adapt to change". If we were to plot that on a two-dimensional graph, we would get something like this:

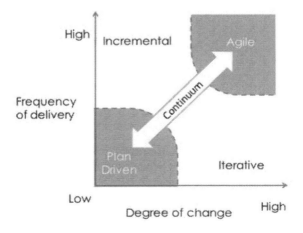

Figure 2.2: "Iterative" vs. "Incremental" vs. "Agile" (Image source: https://www.axelos.com)

On the continuum from plan-driven approaches (lower-left) to Agile approaches (upper-right), there are different degrees of delivery (incremental) and degrees of change (iterative). Techniques that achieve both high degrees of delivery and high degrees of adaptability are called "Agile".

2.12 "Blended" vs. "Hybrid"

Now, that's just too simplistic. In the real world, we don't just use one approach; we almost always combine different techniques. To help understand the different combinations, we've settled on some working definitions.

Blended Agile is the combination of two or more established Agile methods, techniques, or frameworks. Let's depict some key pointers of "Blended vs. Hybrid":

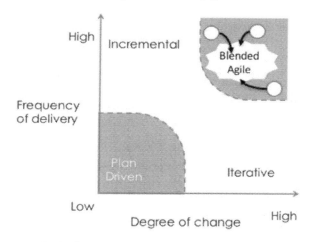

Figure 2.3: Blended" vs. "Hybrid" (Image source: https://www.axelos.com)

That is, adding some Kanban and WIP limits to your Sprints would be a "Blended" approach. Alternatively, maybe you want to "blend" an information radiator with your continuous delivery status. For many Agile practitioners, that's easy to understand. We combine known adaptive-aggressive techniques to improve what we do:

Blended = Agile + Agile = Better Agile

What if we're unable to use these various techniques just yet? What if there are either constraints or demands that require some non-Agile elements? Well, in those cases, you should consider the "Hybrid."

2.13 "Hybrid Agile"

Hybrid Agile is the combination of Agile methods with other non-Agile techniques. Let's depict some key pointers of "Hybrid Agile":

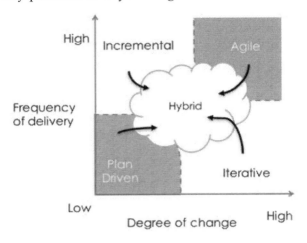

Figure 2.4: *Hybrid Agile (Image source: https://www.axelos.com)*

For example, a detailed requirements effort, followed by sprints of incremental delivery would be a "Hybrid Approach". Likewise, frequent iterative prototyping of a design, followed by a single plan-driven implementation would be a "Hybrid Approach".

Here, the idea is to take a non-Agile approach and inject some Agile techniques to address a specific issue or opportunity:

Hybrid = non-Agile + Agile = something in between that makes sense

2.14 When Should We Use Hybrid Approaches?

Just like anything else in the world, there is a right reason and a wrong reason to do something. To be clear, the wrong reason for combining techniques is to keep up with the Joneses. "Doing Agile techniques" is not the goal. The goal is to deliver the right business outcome using the right techniques.

Here are two scenarios:

1.   **HYBRID AS FIT-FOR-PURPOSE:** For lower-risk profile projects, use plan-driven approaches to look for lower costs. For higher-risk projects, use iterative and incremental activities to resolve any issue(s). For speed-to-market projects, an incremental approach will be a fit-for-purpose solution.

Finally, in order to navigate complex environments, agile techniques may have the overall outcomes although they have higher initial overhead. Each has their own strength, and the right use/mix will produce maximum outcome.

2. **HYBRID AS TRANSITION-TO-AGILE:** For large organizations, teams need to follow a phase-wise approach over the big bang approach. Being Agile is the key rather than doing Agile.

Every project has different needs. For those finding themselves in a mostly plan-driven environment, a hybrid approach can be a transition to more adaptability and delivery. For those already delivering and adapting aggressively, blending in some new techniques can raise the bar even higher.

Don't simply declare, "We're Agile"; the reality is that you're almost always using a combination of techniques. Instead, a better strategy would be to stop and think about which approaches would be best suitable for where we are and what we want to achieve.

2.15 Lessons Learnt from the Agile Leadership Team Journey

The journey of the Agile leadership team in this experience report provides many learnings. Here's a list of the key learnings of my experience:

- Stay focused on your shared goal and be explicit about it. This helps agree on the next action, especially when you're facing a conflict of interests.

- Be prepared for the moment that your culture actually changes. An Agile leadership team has a lot of impact on the Agile culture on the work floor. This means the Agile leadership team has to stay aligned with that culture.

- Know who you work for and respect them. Always ask yourself, "What is the impact on the autonomy of the people when I do this?"

- Never stop evaluating. Don't wait to take action. Just an experiment could be fine to improve, even if you think you're doing well already.

- The agenda of your meeting matters. A lot. It has major impact on the conversation you're having and the decisions you're taking.

2.16 What's the Point of a Story Point? - Story Points and Their Interpretation

Story points are estimates of effort as influenced by the amount of work, complexity, risk, and uncertainty. "When we estimate with story points, we assign a point value to each item. The raw values we assign are unimportant; what matters is the relative values." A story that is assigned a 2 should be twice as much as a story that is assigned a 1. It should also be two-thirds of a story that is estimated as 3 story points:

Figure 2.5: Story points (Image Source: https://www.mountaingoatsoftware.com)

The product backlog is a collection of product requirements (stories, epics, and themes) that delivers value as a whole. The scope of the product or size of the product backlog is the sum of the points of all user stories (of all sizes) in the backlog. The completion of the backlog for a release is tracked by the key metric called the release burn-down. With time/days on the x-axis and the total planned story points for the release on the y-axis, the burn-down shows the rate at which the team is burning these story points. It's obvious that the faster the team burns down these story points, the sooner they'll reach the goal (release goal).

We're not delving into the details of how to estimate and what these numbers should be (linear vs. non-linear series or Fibonacci numbers). The focus of this topic is to discuss how these points affect the life of a scrum team (development team, scrum master, and product owner).

A story adds *"value"* by delivering functionality that the business has asked for and can/will use depending on whether the story is a part of a potentially shippable product increment (and whether the business has requested the increment to be made available in production). The product backlog, a collection of stories, in turn, delivers the *"value as a whole"* or the product to the market to get the business returns on their investment. So, the point here is that a story point is "some value" to the business in terms of functionality.

2.16.1 Stakeholders' Perceptions

What are our stakeholders' perceptions about these points? And how do these perceptions affect the scrum master and the development team?

2.16.1.1 Team Focus

Should the focus be purely on burning points to reach the milestone?

If the team's focus is on anything but delivering value by burning points and meeting the definition of done, the product/release is on a journey that's going to be bitter for the team. More often than not, stakeholders (program/delivery/engagement managers, business sponsors, etc.) purely look at the rate at which the team is burning story points sprint after sprint; their focus is usually on attaining a velocity that will help ensure that the release dates are met (and, in turn, that the flow of funds is maintained).

2.16.1.2 Technical Debt

Does attaining a specific velocity or burning some points ensure that the team is not carrying any technical debt and is also following XP practices (like code refactoring or continuous integration)?

Technical debt, no refactoring, and little/no focus on technical excellence slows down the team by adding to work (more than just functional requirements) that will need to be completed to ensure that a product is both top of the class and gives the business a competitive edge in the market. Last but not least, it affects agility in the long run.

2.16.1.3 Value Delivered

So how should we look at story points?

Focus on getting the story points accepted and pushed out to production (or at least a production-like environment) rather than just completing stories and achieving story point/velocity targets. A team's velocity will fluctuate over release cycles, and fewer story points achieved in one sprint will get balanced out by more that are completed in a future sprint. In the end, it will all average out. Teams should be motivated to deliver stories without accumulating technical debt, while focusing on technical excellence and delivering value.

2.17 Kanban or Scrum? – The Best FIT for Your Organization

Over the years, I have observed management folks debate about the use of Scrum, Kanban, or possibly a combination of the two for software development projects. Sometimes, rational decisions are based on past experience, and sometimes people go with their gut feeling. Other Agile methods available in the market include Crystal, Dynamic Systems Development Method, and Feature-Driven Development, but Scrum and Kanban are, unarguably, the most popular frameworks used in software development. For the purpose of this article, I will focus on Kanban and Scrum.

I have purposely not listed Lean and XP as separate Agile frameworks. In my opinion, XP is closely related to Scrum, and the engineering practices mentioned in XP are used in some way in all Agile frameworks. So, using XP engineering practices becomes a necessity in these contexts. Lean can be considered as the mother of all Agile frameworks, and its principles are invariably used. Some frameworks give them credit directly, whereas others mention them or are indirectly inspired by them. It is important to understand the contexts in which Scrum or Kanban can be used, ensuring that the best results can be achieved over time.

Let's start with the definitions of Scrum and Kanban.

2.17.1 What is Scrum?

The Scrum framework, at its very core, can be defined as following the scientific method of empiricism. It follows an inspect-and-adapt cycle. Scrum uses a heuristic approach and the concept of self-organization to deal with unpredictability and solving complex problems. The Scrum framework has special roles specifically designed to effectively implement Scrum in its true nature.

2.17.2 What is Kanban?

Kanban provides a way to visualize the current flow of work to balance demand with available capacity and reduce bottlenecks in the system. Kanban is based on the following principles:

- **Visualize the workflow:** People are visual beings, and they like to see things in sequence. A sequence can be defined as a list of activities that treats a piece of data or work item that changes its nature to give an acceptable output. Seeing all the work items in context of each other can be informative, and that's the natural way our brains work.

- **Limit the amount of Work In Progress (WIP):** We all know the bad effects of piling up too much work. It has been shown that, as humans, we can only effectively work on one item at a time. Context switching can be dangerous to the workflow. It wastes time and reduces productivity. Limiting WIP helps balance the flow-based approach so that teams don't commit to and start too much work at once.

- **Manage flow:** It is important to review the flow from time to time; it must be managed and monitored to help identify and reduce waste. Managing the flow increases the speed and improves the system.

- **Make policies explicit:** It is important to review the exit criteria for each state in the workflow and only allow work items to pass if they meet the criteria.

- **Improve collaboratively:** When teams have a shared understanding of theories about work, workflow, process, and risk, they are more likely to build a shared comprehension of a problem and suggest improvement actions that can be agreed on by consensus.

2.17.3 Kanban versus Scrum: A Thoughtful Comparison

The key element of building an Agility is a mindset. The following table can help understand the type of mindset shift expected from different Agile process framework(s):

	Kanban	Scrum
1	Kanban focuses on the existing workflow.	Scrum creates a new workflow.
2	No prescribed roles: the development team works in close coordination with the stakeholders.	Prescribed roles: product owner, scrum master, and development team.
3	Timeboxing is optional, but it can be applied to keep a check on work item sizes and help predict the work completion.	Timeboxing is compulsory.
4	No prescribed ceremonies: some, like the daily stand-up, retrospective, etc., can happen, but they need not follow cadence.	Prescribed ceremonies: sprint planning, sprint retrospective, daily stand-up, sprint review, backlog refinement. A cadence is mandatory.
5	Continuous flow — either a one-piece flow or a batch delivery.	This is always a timeboxed delivery of batch work items.
6	Focus on finishing the existing work rather than starting new work.	Focus on starting new work in every new sprint.
7	New work is pulled when old work is completed.	New work is pushed.
8	Changes can be made at any time in the whole cycle. A Kanban system can deal with changing priorities.	Scrum resists changes to the existing work items in the existing sprint. If changes are made, the old items are trashed or pushed back to the product backlog.
9	The product backlog is maintained.	The product backlog is maintained.
10	Kanban focuses on making policies explicit (exit criteria for the items to move from the current state to the next state).	Scrum focuses on the definition of Done (exit criteria for the items to move from the sprint to the Done state).

11	Focus on reducing cycle time and lead time for the items in progress. This is a primary measure of success for the teams.	Focus on velocity (story points, number of completed stories in a sprint).
12	The inspect-and-adapt cycle takes place at the daily stand-ups. These rapid feedback loops help identify and remove waste activities in the system. Retrospectives are not held in a specific cadence, but they contribute to the feedback loops.	The inspect-and-adapt cycle takes place during the sprint at the daily stand-ups and at the end of the sprint in the retrospective.
13	Focus on reducing variability by breaking work items and keeping them of nearly equal size.	Does not focus on reducing variability. Work items ranging from small to big are picked up in the sprint.
14	Absolute estimation takes place in terms of person-hours or ideal days.	Estimation happens at two levels: In backlog refinement, relative estimation in terms of story points or t-shirt sizes. In sprint planning, absolute estimation takes place in terms of person-hours or ideal days.
15	The focus is never on using the available capacity. However, WIP limits are introduced so that team members are not concurrently working on multiple items.	The focus is on using the available capacity of team members in a sprint.
16	The focus is on reducing system waste and improving value-added activities to improve the cycle time and lead time.	Within the prescribed framework, items are not picked up if they have less clarity, reducing wasted effort.
17	Kanban can be applied at the program and portfolio levels. It goes beyond software development teams and can be applied to the whole organization to improve operational effectiveness.	Scrum was initially focused on just software delivery and was not applied to program and portfolios — this has begun to change.

Table 2.1: Kanban Vs. Scrum: A thoughtful comparison

2.17.4 Project Recommendations

Let's look at some key pointers of project recommendations. We've said that agile is a mindset, not a specific set of practices, and many agile teams end up tailoring their agile methodology to their own circumstances.

2.17.4.1 Greenfield Projects (new)

Greenfield projects are the ones that start from zero. They have a fresh appeal and are clean-slate development. The work carried out in such projects does not follow prior work, and there is no dependency on legacy code. For such projects, one can use Scrum or Kanban. However, a lot has to be done before beginning any implementation of the business requirements. Let's see how Scrum and Kanban can help implement new projects.

2.17.5 Setting Up of the Architectural Runway

This is the backbone of product implementation. The architectural features can be completed as spikes or technical items even before implementing business features.

2.17.5.1 Scrum Implementation

Scrum sprints can be used to achieve this. While using Scrum, these implementations can happen in Sprint -2, -1, and 0, respectively:

Sprint	Requested Business Features	Done Features (Business User Stories)	Architectural Features (Spikes/ Technical Requirements)	Throughput (BUS+TR)
Sprint -2	0	0	9	9
Sprint -1	0	0	11	11
Sprint 0	0	0	8	8

Table 2.2: Sample Scrum execution: Running sprints for setting up the architectural runway

2.17.5.2 Kanban Implementation

In Kanban, technical requirements can traverse the workflow in a timeboxed manner. The timebox can be agreed upon by the team and the stakeholders.

2.17.6 Clarifying the Product Roadmap

The product management team must oversee the product road map. The product owner or product manager must also ensure that the product meets the bare minimum requirements or Minimum Viable Product (MVP). Moreover, the roadmap ensures that the product is consistently evolving and meets customer expectations. Techniques such as user story mapping6, product vision board7, product canvas8, and impact mapping9 can help identify the MVP. After the MVP has been decided, features can be distributed as user stories. This journey can be considered the *discovery phase*.

2.17.6.1 Scrum Implementation

Scrum sprints can be run to deliver the business features in continuous and predictable batch transfers. The discovery phase can be run as sprints (Scrum implementation) in the newly setup software workflow. Start on the implementation of business features after the architecture stories are completed:

Sprint	Requested Business Features	Done Features (Business User Stories)	Architectural Features (Spikes/Technical Requirements)	Throughput (BUS+TR)
Sprint 1	Discovery Phase	5	0	5
Sprint 2	Discovery Phase	4	0	4
Sprint 3	Discovery Phase	7	0	7

Table 2.3: Sample Scrum execution: Running sprints to implement the product roadmap

2.17.6.2 Kanban Implementation

Using the Kanban system, the discovery phase features can be implemented to get the MVP right.

2.17.7 Creating and Testing a Working Prototype

As common practice, many organizations ensure that they prepare the skeleton of the product (with basic evolving architecture), put some features on top of it, and then test it for integration and system performance. This is usually more than a prototype, but by doing this activity, the team can ensure that the system works flawlessly, would effectively evolve over time, and has less technical debt.

2.17.7.1 Scrum Implementation

Using sprints, a combination of business features and architecture features can be implemented:

Sprint	Requested Business Features	Done Features (Business User Stories)	Architectural Features (Spikes/Technical Requirements)	Throughput (BUS+TR)
1	0	0	4	4
2	0	0	6	6
3	4	4	-	4
4	2	2	-	2

Table 2.4: Sample Scrum execution: Running sprints to implement the working prototype

2.17.7.2 Kanban Implementation

Using Kanban, a combination of business features and architecture features can be implemented as a continuous flow.

2.17.7.3 Brownfield Projects (Enhancement or Maintenance)

As the system matures, there are challenges related to system performance and technical debt in addition to adding new features.

2.17.8 Scrum Implementation

Regular sprints can be taken up to deliver features, but it becomes difficult to take up technical debt (production issues or internal defects) in the sprints. The general expectation of the **Product Owner (PO)** is to get developers to cultivate features (user stories) in a sprint. Hence, less or no importance is given to technical debt. It is also important to determine the frequency of the incoming work items (tickets). While using Scrum, the team can only have a specific capacity per sprint. So, in a busy season (high frequency of tickets), the Scrum team cannot accommodate additional tickets because of their bandwidth. If they are asked to do so, they recalibrate their sprint duration to extend their capacity. That said, recalibration of sprint length is not a good idea. The team rhythm is broken. In low seasons (low frequency of tickets), the Scrum team struggles to fill up their existing capacity because the influx of tickets is not high.

Over time, the PO and the development team come to a consensus that they would perform sprints that deliver business features tickets and technical debt tickets. They distribute the business features tickets and technical debt tickets in percentage and then commit on sprint work accordingly:

Sprint	Season	Requested Business Features	Done Features (Business User Stories)	Technical Debt (Production Issues, Internal Bugs)	Throughput
1	Low	2	2	8	10
2	Low	3	3	7	10
3	Busy	15	6	3	9
4	Busy	18	5	4	9
5	Low	14	7	3	10
6	Low	8	8	2	10

Table 2.5: Sample mix of features and technical debt in sprints

Over time, when maturity exists between the stakeholders and development team, they can pick a business feature (even ticket) and technical debt (odd tickets). This brings a balance to the system.

2.17.9 Kanban Implementation

Kanban is based on the philosophy of continuous flow; so, adjusting business features and technical debt becomes easy. A Kanban workflow works well with tickets being received with any frequency. Work tickets can be categorized as Expedite, Standard, or Intangible. This categorization makes it simple for the development team to decide when items have to be picked up urgently and have high importance over others. Those who decide the priority of work tickets can put their items in the Expedite or Standard lane and have the tickets continuously delivered.

The use of Scrum and Kanban comes with its own advantages and disadvantages. It is up to the management to build a team based on an Agile framework and reap the benefits over time. However, it should be understood that no framework or method can be a silver bullet for delivery; every implementation evolves over time.

References

1. "11th Annual State of Agile Report," VersionOne, April 6, 2017, **https://explore.versionone.com/state-of-agile/versionone-11th-annual-state-of-agile-report-2**.

2. "Extreme Programming," eGlossary, **https://www.agilealliance.org/glossary/xp/#q=~(filters~(postType~(~'post~'aa_book~'aa_event_session~'aa_experience_report~'aa_glossary~'aa_research_paper~'aa_video)~tags~(~'xp))~searchTerm~'~sort~false~sortDirection~'asc~page~1)**.

3. David Hawks, "7 Principles of Lean Software Development," Agile Velocity, **https://agilevelocity.com/lean/7-principles-of-lean-software-development/**.

4. Figure 1, **https://www.scrum.org/**.

5. Julia Wester, "Going Beyond the Quick Wins of Visualization," Everyday Kanban, October 1, 2017, **http://www.everydaykanban.com/**.

6. "User Story Mapping: Story Mapping Is a Better Way to Work with Agile User Stories," J. Patton Associates, **http://jpattonassociates.com/user-story-mapping/**.

7. Roman Pichler, "The Product Vision Board," **http://www.romanpichler.com/tools/vision-board/**.

8. Roman Pichler, "The Product Canvas," **http://www.romanpichler.com/tools/product-canvas/**.

9. Impact Mapping, **https://www.impactmapping.org/**.

2.18 KANBAN Push and Pull Implementations of Agile Methods

Scrum and Kanban carry out work in different ways: The former works on a push model, whereas the latter adopts a pull mechanism. A Kanban system is a *"pull"* system where demand and capacity are balanced using explicit WIP limits. Scrum is also a *"pull"* system in which a development team pulls a small batch of work into the sprint based on its estimate of how much work it can complete in the given timebox.

Scrum works because the team is self-organizing. No one can tell the team how to do its work or dictate how much work will be completed in a sprint.

Ref: **https://www.frontrowagile.com/blog/posts/94-is-kanban-always-a-pull-system#:~:text=Scrum%20is%20also%20a%20%E2%80%9Cpull,the%20team%20is%20self%2Dorganising**.

The idea behind this way of working is that we are limiting variability to the maximum of a sprint length. For this reason, we prophesize that there will be no change to scope once the sprint starts.

2.18.1 Scrum Pushes

Scrum teams work in a series of sprints, which are generally two weeks in length. Each sprint is accompanied by a sprint planning meeting, which is run by the Scrum master and attended by the product owner and the development team. Together, they select high-priority items from the product backlog that the delivery team believes it can commit to delivering in a single sprint. The selected items are the sprint backlog.

For the next two weeks, the development team focuses on working through the items in the sprint backlog. It's common practice for Scrum teams to use a board (Scrum board/Agile board or Kanban board) to track the progress of work. During the sprint cycle, the Scrum team meets for 15 minutes daily to identify impediments or blockers. At the end of the sprint, the work completed during the sprint is packaged for release. Any incomplete items are returned to the product backlog. The sprint ends with two rituals: sprint review (when the team showcases the increment/working product that has been developed), and the sprint retrospective (an opportunity for the Scrum team to inspect itself and create a plan for improvements to implement during the next sprint). This is Scrum.

2.18.1.1 Kanban Pulls

Kanban does a few things differently. It works entirely on the pull mechanism. There is no two-week sprint, and it's a continuous process. So, there is no sprint backlog.

The pull system in Kanban occurs differently, through WIP (Work In Progress) limits. Each column (Build, Test, Done) on the Kanban board has WIP limits related to the team's capacity. Generally, it is advisable to keep WIP less than the team size. It is an example only. It also illustrates how it transitions from one stage to the next, and how the transitioned state gets replenished with a new item to ensure a continuous flow with minimum waste.

When the testing of a feature is complete, the corresponding ticket moves to the Done column. The empty column is a signal to pick another ticket from the previous column. That's the pull. Similarly, when the Build column is almost empty, it's a signal to the development team to select another high-priority item from the product backlog; that's the pull again.

Like Scrum, Kanban has many rituals, although the naming is slightly different — daily stand-ups, demos for stakeholders, and retrospectives. We can now clearly understand how Scrum and Kanban are different. Neither Scrum nor Kanban is as prescriptive as it may first appear. High-performance teams know what works best for them and flex the systems accordingly.

2.19 Agile Impacts on QA Managers

We now see one industry after another restructuring their organizations toward Agile practices. No verticals (or at least fewer verticals) is the mantra now. This is because Scrum and other Agile approaches have proven that the lesser distance that information has to travel, the more accurate it remains and the more definite the result. Now, working teams interact more with the business and product teams.

This has impacted most managerial roles. As part of the QA industry, I have observed the following shifts required from QA managers. The key element of building an Agility is a mindset. This table helps understand the type of mindset shift expected from different stakeholders:

Actions	What was done	What is to be done
Test strategy and test plan documents	This has now become more obsolete because test strategy, planning, and other testing SLAs are set at iteration levels. Though these documents are drafted and closed at the initial stage of projects, estimates are seen to be changing once the QA activity actually commences.	Shifting the focus onto quicker deliverables is preferred over following the plan. Keep all the stakeholders informed and begin the actual work that requires change of plan. Let the reauthoring and approvals of test strategy and test planning happen parallelly.

Reports	Daily, weekly, and monthly status reports were sent through emails to managers and senior managers. This is actually referred to as effort not required.	Since Agile, SDET, and DevOps are all trending in industry, reports have transformed from one-time information to all-time information, meaning that no emails are required. DevOps tools have emerged to capture the progress of all programming, UI design, and QA at the same location (like comments in a Jira ticket). Tools have come with the option of generating and saving customized reports. The actual intention is that anyone can access those reports. However, we still follow the traditional culture of emailing reports after extracting them from the tool.
Point of contact	Earlier, vendors, or clients were managed by managerial positions. They would remain the point of contact and distribute information to the team. Agile has broken this down, recommending that all the levels of the workforce directly interact with the others concerned for faster results.	This is one of the primary reasons for the QA manager role to fade away. QA managers should probably simply facilitate conversations and involve themselves in situations like preventing risk, providing solutions, or recommending practices.
Work prioritization and allocation	Usually the test lead, and at times, the test managers, prioritize the tasks and send them to the team. Agile, however, advocates that a good team is a self-responsible and self-organized team.	Since the team now communicates directly with the stakeholders, they are in a position to analyze priorities and can pick up tasks accordingly. So, the leads and managers are now restricted only to monitoring and getting involved only if the team faces any challenges.

Table 2.6: Agile impact on QA managers

In addition to people management, skill set management, and resource management, leaders today must build skills in tool integration and process solutions. The demand for techno-functional leaders has already increased.

2.20 Recognizing the Five Symptoms of a Poor Backlog - A Two-part Solution

Let's look at some key pointers to recognizing the "*Five Symptoms of a Poor Backlog*". Your description may vary, depending on what part of the principle stands out most for you, but the following are the possible abbreviations.

2.20.1 Understanding the Backlog

The backlog is a single source of prioritized development objectives, tracked either by sticky notes or a backlog tool. The backlog provides a clear path for the business and IT when considering what's next for development.

Agile teams continuously run short iterations to deliver working software, and the backlog is the starting point that indicates what to sign up next. It is important that this backlog has clear, prioritized value objectives. If it fails to give direction for feature or product development, chances are that the Agile team will not deliver what the customer demands. It is the fuel that runs the sprints and the single source from which business can get an idea of what remains for future feature work, contributing to better decision making.

Assuming that your team does not have a backlog, how will they plan their sprint and how will the business know what will be delivered next? I have identified five symptoms of a poorly-defined backlog, which indicate that the team is not working effectively and needs improvement.

2.20.2 Five Symptoms of a Poor Backlog

There are various early indicators that your product owner is struggling to provide clear direction to the team. If the direction is not clear, the results will not be promising, and ultimately, the business will struggle, impacting the organization's profitability. In my opinion, it is important to watch for symptoms as early as possible so that proper course correction can be done to improve the entire process.

2.20.2.1 Symptom 1: Poor Planning

When a Scrum team struggles to define a solid plan during the sprint planning session and the product owner is unable to provide clear direction, this is the first indication that the team has a serious problem.

In this case, the result of the planning meeting will be either no planning or objectives that do not have a clear value defined. I call this impulsive sprint planning. The sprint was planned without any business inputs, and it was held only for namesake. It is not a winning situation for the organization because it will not get a good return on investment. It will not only affect spending but also the timing and opportunity to beat the competition.

If the team is in the early stages of its Agile movement, it is acceptable to have this type of situation for a couple of sprints. However, it is important to recognize this symptom and have an open dialog with the product owner to resolve the problem.

2.20.2.2 Symptom 2: Not Enough Detail

When your Agile team is conducting its sprint planning, do they elicit the required details of the stories? If not, your Scrum team is running the risk that they will not be able to deliver what they commit and will ruin the team's credibility.

Ideally, during backlog grooming, someone from the IT team is involved in capturing the right level of details needed for the development team to be effective during its sprint planning. It's common to not have IT representation during backlog grooming. If you feel this is the typical situation for your team, consider having your tech lead or architect work with the product owner before sprint planning.

2.20.2.3 Symptom 3: More than 20% Churn in Objectives

If you are running two-week sprints and your business objectives are constantly shuffling, it indicates that your backlog is not solid. Your product owner has to work hard to lock down the objectives. Some degree of churn is expected, but if it is more than 20%, the product owner deserves feedback.

Showing agility to the business is important, but if this churn is frequent, curtail it. It's okay to have churn to support the business, but course correction is required if it is the result of poor backlog planning. All types of changes have a cost associated with them. The product owner should be able to recognize this pain and work toward solidifying the backlog grooming process.

2.20.2.4 Symptom 4: The Customer Did Not Like the Feature

If your customers do not like a recently released feature and provide feedback, this is a sign that the customer's voice was not considered while hardening the backlog, or that customers were never consulted during that process. It is important to listen to customers during the backlog grooming process to help the team deliver the right product and also save a lot of money in developing non–value-added objectives.

In the end, a feature is developed for the customer, and they should be at the center of the requirements gathering and consulted early in the process. If you are frequently hearing feedback from the customer about a feature not meeting their expectations, why not involve them in the process? This can take the form of inviting some of the customers for the demo so that course correction can be made based on their feedback. Customers will also feel engaged during development.

2.20.2.5 Symptom 5: Running Out of Funds

Is your objective always running out of funds? It's not uncommon to see software development objectives run out of funds because of ever-evolving business expectations. It is the product owner's job to find out what requirement is a must and what is a nice-to-have.

If a team investing a lot of its time in nice-to-have requirements later finds that it is running out of money to deliver the must-haves, it is a bad indicator. Instead, the team must deliver the must requirements first and, if time and budget permit, focus on the nice-to-have ones. The next time you find that your team is running out of money to deliver the must requirements, consider that they are not getting the proper direction. Coach the product owner on prioritization by entering into a simple dialog or setting expectations for the individual.

2.20.3 Effects of a Poor Backlog

The product backlog plays a major role in product development. If it is not properly defined, the development team struggles with delivering objectives that matter to the business and directly impact the organization's profitability. It is a driver for successful product development, and reaching the organization's goal is impossible if this direction is missing.

The product backlog also plays a critical role in engaging the Scrum team. If the product owner can effectively articulate the business challenges to the Scrum team, they can point the Scrum team in a positive direction. However, if the business objectives are uncertain or there is no rationale behind some of them, the Scrum team is unmotivated because it is unable to understand what value they are providing and how they will impact customers.

The repercussions of a poor backlog are high, and an organization cannot afford this situation for too long. As soon as any symptoms occur, it must correct the process. The product backlog should be the center of development, and we have to always keep it current and meaningful.

2.20.4 Applying a Two-part Solution

If you are in your early days of Agile adoption and have one or more symptoms of a poor backlog, try a two-part approach that could push the team in the right direction; they will think about a potential solution. The goal is to have an entire team—the business and IT team—work together and show agility to beat the competition and provide the best solution to customers.

2.20.4.1 Part 1: Set Expectations

The product owner is the voice of the customer and is closely tied to the delivery team. So, set the right expectation with the product owner. Ask the product owner to apply a priority order to the backlog, with a clear definition of ready and defined stories and acceptance criteria. Developers and business stakeholders should be able to understand the criteria easily, and the product owner should provide the proper insights whenever required. The product owner should also define which story is a must for the feature and which story should be considered a nice-to-have. When these stories have been identified, it's easy for the development team to start working on the backlog.

2.20.4.2 Part 2: Schedule Regular Backlog Grooming Sessions

It's typical for a new Agile team to have a product owner who struggles to define the priority order of a backlog. Everyone is confused about where and how to start. To solve this problem, run a common backlog grooming meeting in which the product owner, product manager, and someone from the technical team meet regularly (weekly is recommended). This team should discuss the current business opportunities and potential IT solutions, and they should rearrange the backlog according to the current business priority. This meeting should provide a solid foundation for the backlog grooming and enable the product owner to provide clear direction to the Scrum team.

The meeting should not only focus on the current and next sprint but also continuously work toward the future direction of the product. The product backlog sheds light on the path of product development.

2.20.5 Conclusion

It is impossible to remain competitive in the market with a poor backlog. It is common to have struggled with the backlog grooming. However, for the organization to remain profitable and meet the original intention of being Agile, it's important to recognize the symptoms of a poor backlog, embrace the ensuing challenges, and move in the right direction.

2.21 What Agile Can and Cannot Do - A Journey Worth Understanding

Agile is a relatively new way of directing software development that has been gaining momentum in the IT industry. Many organizations are adopting Agile practices, blindly trusting that the method can solve all their issues. However, it is not a magic pill that will solve the problems of the organization. It is indeed a mindset shift and a big, positive step toward software development excellence. However, nothing will be automatically solved. By following Agile practices, you will recognize early indicators of problems that you can solve before they become too big or complex.

Let's talk about what Agile can and cannot do for several common software development problems.

2.21.1 Scheduling

The project schedule is one of the major pain points in software development. Many project schedules overrun, which ultimately results in missed market opportunities and a negative return on investment. Many teams shift into Agile hoping that their schedule overruns will be solved.

- **What Agile can do:** As your development iteration will be small, you can mitigate your risks by prioritizing only the required set of features. A powerful strategy is to complete the minimum required features and go to market quickly to gain the most market share. Also, with this strategy, you can release features fast and provide value to your customers much earlier in the development lifecycle. In the current method, you might be releasing once in every 3-6 months, but you can release more frequently if you transition to Agile.

- **What Agile cannot do:** In Agile, you gain an insight into your project schedule so that you can make the required changes on priority to control the project timeline. It is unrealistic to expect that your team will never run into scheduling issues once you train them in any Agile method. If you feel that it is taking too long to complete feature work, reduce the number of items that are not required and ensure that only the required tasks are done. With Agile's short iterations, it is possible to know how the team is progressing and what the current schedule looks like.

By gaining an insight into the project schedule, you will have opportunities to make the required changes that are more important for the business. However, this insight will not directly protect you from schedule overruns, and it is your responsibility to recognize scheduling problems early and mitigate the risks. Even after adopting Agile, identify any opportunities to make course corrections if you face a scheduling problem. Although Agile gives you early insight, it is your responsibility to solve the problem.

2.21.2 Prioritizing

Businesses are dynamic, and it is next to impossible for the business team to lock down priorities for the next year or beyond. This was a common problem before Agile; many projects developed feature X when the business team was expecting feature Y, or they found that feature X was no longer relevant to the product.

- **What Agile can do:** You can frequently change the priorities that make sense to the business. The business team will feel more confident about what is being developed and that it will meet their expectation. You can reduce waste almost immediately because of frequent interactions with business. If you determine at the end of the cycle that the team applied the wrong implementation, it will cost more to fix that scenario than if the misjudgment had been identified earlier in the cycle.

- **What Agile cannot do:** The ability to change priorities frequently can be rewarding as well as disconcerting because business might change their minds and make many changes that will ultimately increase costs. Educate your business stakeholders to prioritize the right features or at least establish a structure in which a thoroughly scrutinized backlog is prioritized.

We need to recognize that prioritizing is a way of supporting the work and should be carefully applied. If it is not, it will create churn for the development team, resulting in waste. Transitioning to Agile will not solve your problem of constantly shifting priorities, but it will enable you to tackle changes more efficiently.

If you have ever faced a situation in which you were not getting anything done even after being Agile, review your backlog. Were you able to give clear direction to the team with the appropriately prioritized backlog? You have the power to support the business by accommodating changing business needs, so this capability should be used wisely. However, having the capability does not mean that you must continually change the requirements. More frequent changes are symptomatic of a product owner who is reluctant to identify or solidify the requirements.

2.21.3 Reducing Costs

Cost is a crucial aspect of any software development project, and it will heavily impact the project's profitability if not handled appropriately. The goal of many organizations is to handle cost efficiently by transitioning to Agile.

- **What Agile can do:** Agile empowers you to change feature priority early in the development cycle, which will enable the business to maximize profit. You can increase cost savings by delaying features that are not required.

Also, one of the goals is to release frequently, which means you are tapping the market early. Identifying issues early on reduces the cost of development, and finding issues late in the development cycle will increase costs.

- **What Agile cannot do:** We should recognize that Agile teams need constant coaching in the early days of adoption and time to settle down. So, we should be ready to invest in that initial cost. The notion that the team will be productive from day one is an unrealistic expectation. In fact, the team can take even a few months to adjust before delivering at their maximum potential. In your early days of adoption, you will see a spike in cost, so prepare for it.

In Agile, you can reduce your rework and provide what is needed for business. If you feel you are not getting what is expected, despite the training and coaching, wait for some time and let the team settle down. Examine your original intention of wanting to be Agile, communicate to your coach and team about expectations, design a realistic plan by when you can see results, and let the team find its own path to excellence. Have faith in your team and be patient during the first step of being Agile.

2.21.4 Tracking Progress

No organization likes to run projects without using an appropriate method to monitor their progress and ensure that the team remains aligned with the original goals.

- **What Agile can do:** There are various metrics available in Agile for tracking progress. Attending daily stand-ups or visiting the whiteboard will give you a current and true picture of the progress.

- **What Agile cannot do:** If you have used traditional ways to collect metrics or have viewed color-coded weekly and monthly reports, you will be disappointed after transitioning to Agile. You will certainly miss your reports. Agile is a more collaborative approach, whereby you must make an effort to attend Agile ceremonies to get the true status or progress of the project.

In Agile, there are more practical ways to gain an insight into the current progress of the project. It is more of a collaborative effort in that it encourages you to frequently interact with team members. Relying on those color-coded reports, which depend on the person who creates them, may not be a true representation of the progress.

2.21.5 Ensuring Team Satisfaction

Team satisfaction is one of the huge benefits of being Agile. Individuals who are engaged and motivated give better results and reduce attrition in the team. Team members will feel connected to each other and challenged by their goal to meet business expectations.

- **What Agile can do:** Agile allows autonomy for the team members. By signing up for what they really would like to work on, they can try new challenges. When members sign up for an objective, they feel committed to it.
- **What Agile cannot do:** Even after adopting it, Agile cannot motivate your team. You must also trust your team to tackle new challenges. Trust is a crucial factor in the success of any team. Do not get in their way; let them explore their own transition and path.

Are you still forcing team members to sign up for objectives after transitioning to Agile? Are you not trusting them to try new things? If your answers are yes, think about changing your approach. Your team members might already be demotivated and feeling that Agile is not working for them. What is stopping you from empowering the team to sign up for its own commitments?

2.21.6 Conclusion

Every organization has its own goals and expectations when transitioning to Agile, but you must strive to identify and resolve problems. The transition to Agile is a mindset shift. When you understand the power of being Agile, you will find answers and simple, workable solutions. It is a journey and a change, which is always hard. Embrace the change and enjoy your Agile journey. You will not regret it.

2.22 Managing Releases in a Scrum Framework

This article presents one way of delivering production-ready code at the end of every sprint. In a scenario in which Scrum teams are actually feature teams engaged in developing, enhancing, or maintaining products, they do not always accomplish a production-deployable product at the end of every sprint.

2.22.1 Ways to Successfully Deliver Production-deployable Code

Instead of highlighting the reasons for unsuccessful sprints, I'll explain the ways to successfully deliver production-deployable code at the end of every sprint.

2.22.1.1 Consolidate Planning

Backlog refinement is a constant activity. Product owners work on the priority and details of their wish list daily. Consolidated planning can be done for getting an overall organizational priority. This is the meeting in which each product owner presents their backlog to the business stakeholders and ensures that individual product backlogs are aligned with the organizational goals. The frequency of these meetings can be every quarter or twice a year. After the consolidated plan is approved, teams begin work on the highest-priority items from this backlog. What teams decide to work on in a sprint becomes the sprint backlog for the Scrum team.

2.22.1.2 Define a Sprint Cadence

Following a regular sprint size is advantageous for teams. Teams get into a rhythm to plan, build, and review at a regular cadence. They have more confidence in the velocity and so, more accuracy in estimations.

2.22.1.3 Practice Continuous Integration

It's important to use continuous integration tools and apply engineering best practices for development teams, especially when there are multiple Scrum teams working on different features for the same product. Follow a branching strategy to handle daily code check-ins and merges to the release branch. Control merges to the release branch by defining the release readiness criteria. Only the code that meets these readiness criteria is merged with the release branch.

2.22.1.4 Define What is Ready

Just like defining the acceptance criteria of a story, you must also define readiness criteria for releasing the story. Acceptance criteria of the story can be extended to include the release readiness criteria. The challenge will be to satisfy all the criteria in the same sprint. The tasks required to build the software will precede the tasks required to package and release it. If they are combined and done together, I would call this a successful DevOps implementation.

2.22.1.5 Assess Release Readiness

At the end of every sprint review, the stories are "done" with development and testing on the daily build. This Done list becomes the backlog for release. The release backlog is reviewed and prepared for production deployment in the subsequent sprint. All the tasks required to get the developed stories to the delivery channel and production deployment are completed during the following sprint:

Timelines		Sprint 1		Sprint 2		Sprint 3		Sprint 4		Sprint 5		Sprint 6		Sprint 1	
Quarter Start -->														Quarter Start -->		
		Week 1	Week 2	Week 1	Week 2	Week 1	Week 2	Week 1	Week 2	Week 1	Week 2	Week 1	Week 2	Week 1	Week 2
Sprint Planning	Quarterly Planning Sprint Planning	Sprint Planning		Sprint Planning		Sprint Planning		Sprint Planning		Sprint Planning		Quarterly Planning Sprint Planning		Sprint Planning	
Release Plan	Release (P1) Readiness Meeting	Production Deployment (P1) Release (P2) Readiness Meeting		Production Deployment (P2) Release (P3) Readiness Meeting		Production Deployment (P3) Release (P4) Readiness Meeting		Production Deployment (P4) Release (P5) Readiness Meeting		Production Deployment (P5) Release (P6) Readiness Meeting		Production Deployment (P6) Release (P1) Readiness Meeting		Production Deployment (P1) Release (P2) Readiness Meeting	

Figure 2.6: Managing a release within sprints (Image Source: https://www.scrumalliance.org)

The purpose of release planning is to commit to a plan for delivering an increment of product value. Release planning is a collaborative effort involving these roles:

- **Scrum Master -** Facilitates the meeting
- **Product Owner** – Ideally from customer, represents a general view of the product backlog
- **Delivery team/Agile team** – Provide insights into technical feasibility and dependencies
- **Stakeholders -** Act as trusted advisors as decisions are made around the release plan

2.23 Agile and Deepawali Celebrations - Implementing Kanban Unconsciously

Deepawali is a famous multi-day festival celebrated in many parts of India, when people eat sweets and burst firecrackers. On this occasion, people want to buy enough firecrackers to cover the time period of the celebrations. They plan carefully in order to be able to buy a variety (some varieties being available in limited quantity) so that the celebration does not feel monotonous -- but they also do not want to end up with leftover, unused firecrackers at the end.

This year, I was particularly struck by the various Kanban practices at work. Using Kanban, we visualize the workflow, limit the work in progress, and manage the flow. In the Diwali scenario, people followed similar practices:

- Visualize the celebrations, including the fireworks
- Manage the inflow for sufficiency (buy enough crackers) while reducing waste (avoid ending up with unused crackers)
- Celebrate the festival (focus on continuous delivery)
- Formulate policies to explode the crackers without causing disturbance to others, and do it before neighbors want to go to sleep
- Continuously learn and consider feedback (from family members engaged in celebrations, as a team) based on the experience (which crackers are good to buy considering the celebrants' age, the time, situation, etc.) so that it can be implemented for improvements in the following celebrations

This is one specific example illustrating my strong feeling that we have been following Kanban practices in many situations without our consciousness of the system. The fact that we already adopt these principles in day-to-day life is part of what makes Kanban appealing and comparatively easy to learn. We can also observe how we already use these principles and extended the practices further as applicable.

2.24 Address Risk with Spikes

A technical necessity in Agile software development, "Spikes" are periods of work undertaken to reduce threats and issues, and "architectural spikes" are iterations used to prove a technological approach. The spikes are blended into the release planning processes.

2.24.1 What is a Spike?

A spike is a research-and-analysis task for a complex epic or story. A complex epic or story cannot be broken or estimated in the right way until the development team investigates the details. A spike addresses the uncertainties around the epic or story. The spike output helps provide the estimate for the original epic or story and unblocks ways to disintegrate the uncertainties.

2.24.2 What causes an Epic or Story to Form a Spike?

While discussing an epic or story in the backlog refinement session—or even before that— the team should form a spike if it realizes any of the following inadequacies or gaps:

- A technical understanding of the story is necessary before the team can assign story points to it in the refinement session.

- The team must gain the necessary knowledge of the user story and remove the risk of potentially applying an unknown technical approach to the iteration, timebox, or sprint.

- The team must attempt various techno-functional solution approaches in the said domain before finalizing an approach for development.

2.24.3 Guidelines for Spikes

As spikes do not directly deliver business value, they should be used only when the team needs clarity about an epic or story. Let's take a look at the guidelines that apply.

2.24.3.1 Make Them Estimable, Demonstrable, and Acceptable

Like stories or epics, spikes are put in the backlog, estimated in person hours, and sized to fit an iteration, timebox, or sprint. If the team is working in Kanban, it should use a timebox of 20 hours maximum for the spike items, which is a ballpark figure and can be adjusted as and when required.

The spike must develop sufficient information to resolve the uncertainty around the understanding and development of the epic or story. The spike outcome must be demonstrable to the team and any other interested parties. This brings transparency to the R&D efforts and helps build collective ownership and shared accountability/responsibility for the key decisions.

2.24.3.2 Time the Spikes

Here and in the following section, I am indebted to the Scaled Agile discussion of spikes at **http://www.scaledagileframework.com/spikes/**. As a spike represents uncertainty in potential epics or user-stories, planning for both the resultant stories and the spikes in the same iteration becomes risky. Even if the spike is a small effort and a quick resolution is likely to be noticed, it can be beneficial to complete a spike and to groom and develop the story in the following iterations.

2.24.3.3 Consider the Exception, Not the Rule

Every user story has some amount of risk and uncertainty that is the nature of development using Agile. The team discovers the appropriate solution through empirical brainstorming session, collaboration, negotiation, and experimentation. This is a pragmatic approach that improves over time. So, in one way, every user-story consists of spike-like activities to identify the techno-functional feasibility and non-functional/functional risk. To learn how to embrace and effectively address this uncertainty is one of the goals of an Agile team. A spike task should be reserved for the critical and larger unknowns.

2.25 Benefits and Barriers to Enterprise Agility

As we have seen, Agile SHIFT defines enterprise agility as the ability of an organization to move and adapt quickly in response to shifting customer and market needs. This definition recognizes that RTO and CTO are quite different expressions of an organization that must work in close association with each other for the benefit of the entire organization.

For an organization to remain competitive and keep up with the accelerating pace of change, it must change:

- The mindset of its people
- Its governance, controls, and processes
- Its expectations
- Its ways of working so that it can:
    o Undergo transformational change
    o Adopt a 'survive, compete, and thrive' mindset
    o Narrow its delta to get closer to where it wants to be
    o Embrace a range of Agile, structured, and hybrid approaches

There are many organizational benefits and barriers to enterprise agility, some of which are listed in this table:

Benefits	Barriers
Greater innovation	Traditional 'silo' mentality
Improvements in productivity	Long established culture
The increased ability to transform	Pressure to deliver this month's objectives
Better organizational change management	Complacency
Growth	Lack of buy-in at all levels
Better protection against disruptors	Outdated procedures, processes, and rules

Table 2.7: Benefits and barriers to enterprise agility

The benefits of enterprise agility to individuals include increased motivation through:

- Working on ideas that they know to be worthwhile
- Working autonomously in self-organizing teams (see Section 9.1.2)
- Becoming better at what they do, developing new skills, and enjoying increased job satisfaction

Your description may vary, depending on what part of the principle stands out most for you, but the above-mentioned are possible abbreviations.

2.26 Multimodal Working

Every organization is unique. Even in the same sector or industry, organizations vary in composition, ethos, culture, and style. They also differ according to their size and working practices as well as the kind of value they create and deliver.

The needs of the people, processes, tasks, tools, and other elements that make up these complex entities need to be understood so that the different ways of working can be made appropriate for those delivering the work and the work itself. This is known as multimodal working.

In Agile SHIFT, the acceptance that an optimized state may include adopting multimodal ways of working is described in *Figure 2.7*:

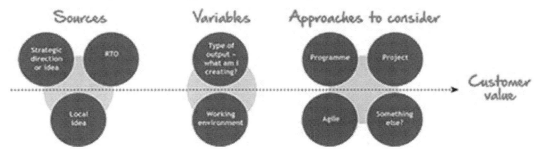

Figure 2.7: Multimodal working (Image source: https://www.axelos.com)

Within one program or change initiative, we might see an Agile project, evidence of Scrum working, a Kanban delivery, and even an unstructured piece of work, all contributing to the initiative. Any or all of these approaches can help deliver customer and user value.

The purpose of Agile SHIFT is to encourage and equip all areas of an organization to become more agile in the most appropriate way. There is a tremendous amount to be gained by embracing a variety of ways of working, developing agility, and becoming better able to both run and change the organization.

2.27 Enterprise Agility and the Creation of Smaller-scale Agility

The Agile SHIFT framework draws on best-practice thinking in Agile approaches to create agility not only at the enterprise level but also at individual and team levels, giving rise to smaller-scale agility.

This agility will develop through:

- A willingness to adopt a multimodal approach at all levels rather than following a single ideology
- Everyone in the organization seeking to be agile in the way they work with and support other teams
- The development of a common transformation terminology across all teams

The principles, practices, roles, and workflow of Agile SHIFT will support the development of this agility.

We've said that agile is a mindset and not a specific set of practices, and many agile teams end up tailoring their agile methodology to their own circumstances.

2.28 Five Dysfunctions of a Team

Patrick Lenrioni, author of The Five Dysfunctions of a Team, lists the following dysfunctions that damage and limit team performance:

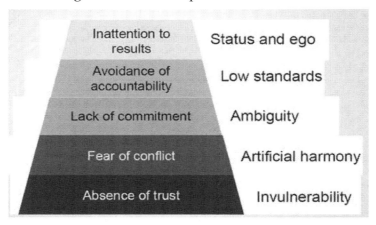

Figure 2.8: *Five dysfunctions of a team (Image source: https://www.axelos.com)*

These dysfunctions stem from avoiding conflict (or constructive disagreement) and not having a safe environment in which it is okay to ask questions. Establishing a safe environment for disagreement is key to success; such an environment allows team members to build a strong commitment to decisions. If team members have such a commitment when they encounter the inevitable obstacles on a project, they will push past the obstacles or find a way around them instead of returning to management with a list of reasons why something cannot be done.

2.29 Top 3 Improvement Practices of Agile

- **Metrics and measures -** A metric is a system of measurement that includes the item being measured (what we measure), the method of measurement (how we measure), and the inherent value associated with the metric (why we measure or what we intend to achieve by this measurement).

- **Point Kaizen -** Kaizen framework (Japanese business philosophy of continuous small incremental improvement of working practices, personal efficiency, etc.), based on 5 S & PDCA practices.

- **Showcase/Retro/Celebrate** – Inspect, adapt, step back, and take feedback, improve, and sustain are the key approaches.

Now, let's look at some additional pointers.

BVC (Big Visual Charts)

Some important pointers:

- Metric
    - o   Cycle time
    - o   Throughput
    - o   Unit cost
    - o   Customer satisfaction
    - o   Team satisfaction
- Issue
- Risk
- Team info

2.30 Example of Value Stream Mapping in Sales on Proposals

Value is a measure of benefit created through the delivery of goods or services. Time value of money is a key concept to be considered. Product owner elevated above the value stream, facilitates the replenishment meeting and risk management policies.

Visualize the Work

Agile is all about delivering value to the customer and delighting them and the stakeholders. Determining customer value involves activities such as:

- Collaborating with customers
- Creating focus groups
- Reducing technical debt

KANBAN – Visualize the work:

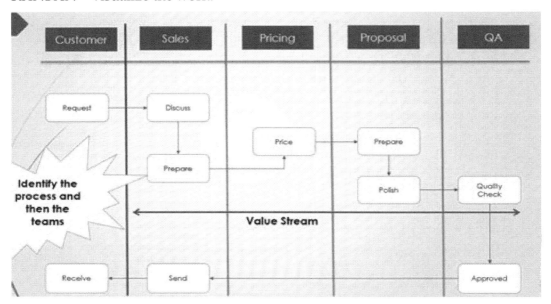

Figure 2.9: *KANBAN – Visualize the work (Image Source: leankanban.com)*

Value Stream Mapping

KANBAN – Value stream mapping:

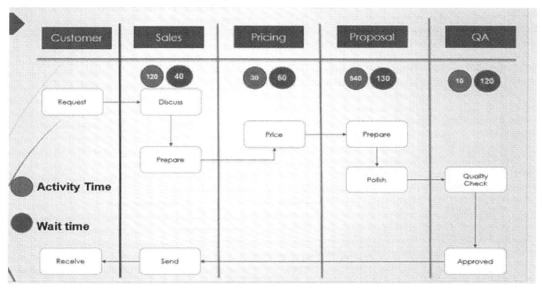

Figure 2.10: KANBAN – Value stream mapping (Image Source: leankanban.com)

Total Cycle Time, Activity Time, and Process Efficiency Calculation

KANBAN – Process efficiency calculation:

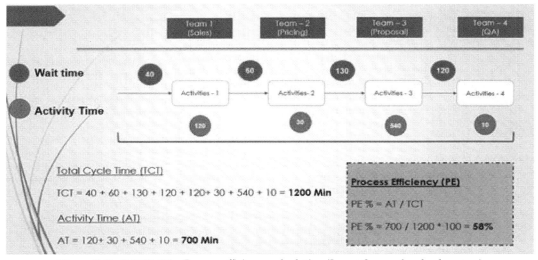

Figure 2.11: KANBAN – Process efficiency calculation (Image Source: leankanban.com)

Conclusion

In this chapter, we mainly discussed:

- Key secrets of Agile Leadership
- Categorization of organizational risks
- Address risks with spikes
- FIT FOR PURPOSE – Kanban / Scrum
- Hybrid Agile
- Enterprise Agility
- Examples of value stream mapping in sales on proposals
- Agile and Deepawali celebrations
- PUSH and PULL implementations of Agile methods
- Agile impacts on QA managers
- Different types of dysfunctions in Agile
- Practice transparency through visualization
- Create a safe environment for experimentation
- Experiment with new techniques and processes
- Share knowledge through collaboration
- Encourage emergent leadership via a safe environment
- Lessons learnt and pragmatic approach to help sustain customer relationships and enhance business/customer delights
- Tricky tips & traps on Agile, Scrum, KANBAN etc.

The scrum masters, product owners, developers, and professionals closely associated with Agile Scrum, Kanban, and XP projects can further improve their knowledge of Agile with valuable pragmatic insights. Entry-level professionals and Agile enthusiasts with relevant experience can also acquire an in-depth knowledge of the concepts discussed in the Agile methodology tutorial.

In the next chapter, you should be able to:

- Understand Agile SCRUM Kanban concept in your personal life as parents or students and understand how to apply field rules for faster performance & better results.
- Understand the tricky tips & traps on Agile, Scrum, KANBAN, etc.

Let's check out some review questions.

Questions

1. **Name the Extreme Programming (XP) technique where one programmer is responsible for the typing/writing of the code, while the other is responsible for the continuous review of the work.**

   a. Planning Game

   b. Coding Technique

   c. Planning Poker

   d. Pair Programming

   e. Planning Technique

2. **Which of the following explains refactoring?**

   a. Code quality improvement

   b. Time saving

   c. Redundancy removal

   d. Minimizes bugs drastically

   e. Rejuvenate obsolete designs

3. **In Extreme Programming (XP), the source code usually goes through 4 levels of completion.**

   Select the correct answer(s).

   a. Build, Ready for DEMO, Broken, Ready to release

   b. Broken, Build, Ready for DEMO, Ready to release

   c. Broken, Build, Ready to release, Ready for DEMO

   d. Build, Ready for DEMO, Ready to release, Broken

   e. Others

4. **In Extreme Programming (XP), pair programming can be correlated with _____.**

   Select the correct answer(s).

   a. Programmer welfare

   b. Fine-scale feedback

   c. Continuous process

   d. Shared understanding

   e. Others

5. **In Extreme Programming (XP), collective code ownership can be correlated with _____.**

    Select the correct answer(s).

    a. Programmer welfare

    b. Fine-scale feedback

    c. Continuous process

    d. Shared understanding

    e. Others

6. **Which technique in code refactoring is used in the following code snippet?**

    Select the correct answer(s).

```
// Before
public class TestOverriding {
    public static void main(String aga[]){
        Parrot bird=new Parrot();
        bird.fly();
    }
}
class Bird{
    private  void eats(){
        System.out.println("......");
    }
}
class Parrot extends Bird{
    public void doStuff(){
        System.out.println("I am parrot , and I am doing stuff");
    }
    public void fly(){
        System.out.println("Bird is flying");
    }
}
class Pigeon extends Bird{
    public void doStuff(){
        System.out.println("I am Pigeon , and I am White");
    }
    public void fly(){
```

```
            System.out.println("Bird is flying");
        }
    }
// After
public class TestOverriding {
    public static void main(String aga[]){
        Parrot bird=new Parrot();
        bird.fly();
    }
}
class Bird{
    private  void fly(){
        System.out.println("Bird is flying");
    }
    private  void eats(){
        System.out.println("......");
    }
}
class Parrot extends Bird{
    public void doStuff(){
        System.out.println("I am parrot , and I am doing stuff");
    }
}
class Pigeon extends Bird{
    public void doStuff(){
        System.out.println("I am Pigeon , and I am White");
    }
}
```

a. Increasing level of abstraction

b. Inline methods

c. Generalization

d. Inline class

e. Others

7. **Which technique in code refactoring is used in the following code snippet?**
   Select the correct answer(s).

```
// Before
int getRating() {
    return(moreThanFiveLateDeliveri s()) ? 2 : 1;
}
boolean moreThanFiveLateDeliveries() {
    return (numberOfLateDeliveries > 5);
}
// After
int getRating() {
  return ((numberOfLateDeliveries > 5) ? 2 : 1);
}
```

   a. Increasing level of abstraction
   b. Inline methods
   c. Generalization
   d. Inline class
   e. Others

8. **In the following code snippet, which technique in code refactoring is being used?**
   Select the correct answer(s).

```
// Before
class Person{
    private string PersonName;
    private string Address;
    public int getTelephoneNumber() { }
}
class telephoneNumber extends Person{
    private int areaCode;
    private int number;
    public int getTelephoneNumber() { }
}
// After
```

```
class Person{
    private string PersonName;
    private string Address;
    private int areaCode;
    private int number;
    public int getTelephoneNumber() { }
}
```

    a.   Increasing level of abstraction

    b.   Inline methods

    c.   Generalization

    d.   Inline classes

    e.   Others

9. **What are the "Pros" of using "Collective code ownership"?**
   Select the correct answer(s).

       a.   Multiple programmers can fix issue

       b.   Only one programmer can fix issue

       c.   Speeds up the development process

       d.   Increases dependency on owner of the code

       e.   Eliminates dependency on owner of the code

10. **Which of the following agendas is NOT true for collective code ownership?**

        a.   Everyone is not responsible for all the code

        b.   Speeds up the development process

        c.   Everyone is not allowed to change any part of the code

        d.   Provides collaboration

        e.   Interlinked with shared understanding

Question Number	Answer	Explanation
1	d	**Correct Answer:** d. Pair programming is when two developers work on the same code together to improve efficiency.
2	a, b, c, e	**Correct Answer:** a, b, c, e. Refactoring is the reorganization of code to make it more organized and is used for code quality improvement, time saving, redundancy removal, and to rejuvenate obsolete designs.

3	b	**Correct Answer:** b. The four levels of completion are broken, build, ready for demo, and ready to release.
4	b	**Correct Answer:** b. In Extreme Programming (XP), pair programming can be correlated with fine-scale feedback.
5	d	**Correct Answer:** d. In Extreme Programming (XP), collective code ownership can be correlated with shared understanding.
6	c	**Correct Answer:** c. Generalization technique of code refactoring is being used here.
7	b	**Correct Answer:** b. Inline methods technique of code refactoring is being used here.
8	d	**Correct Answer:** d. Inline classes technique of code refactoring is being used here.
9	a, c, e	**Correct Answer:** a, c, e Pros of using "Collective code ownership" Speeds up the development process since multiple programmers can fix issue Eliminates dependency on owner of the code
10	a, c	**Correct Answer:** a, c. In collective code ownership, everyone is responsible for all the code. So, everyone is allowed to change any part of the code. Pair programming contributes to this practice. It helps make the code visible to more developers.

CHAPTER 3

Use of Agile for Students and Parents

Introduction

In this chapter, we will mainly cover the following topics. After completing this lesson, you will be able to describe/explain/implement:

- Agile learning vs. traditional learning

- Agile education manifesto

- Agile education principles

- Agile education values

- Agile education roles

- Agile education meetings

- Agile education artefacts

- Agile education sample selection criteria during the screening process

- Self-directed morning checklists for students before going to school

Do you ever worry about not following Agile, Scrum, KANBAN, XP, etc. best practices in your personal life as parents or students? Or are you/your child anxious about your child's admission at school?

In this chapter, you should be able to:

- Understand Agile SCRUM Kanban concept in your personal life as parents or students and how to apply field rules for faster performance & better results
- Understand the tricky tips & traps of Agile, Scrum, KANBAN etc.

Happy learning.

Structure

In this chapter, we will discuss the following topics:
- AGILE LEARNING VS. TRADITIONAL LEARNING
- Agile education manifesto
- Agile education principles
- Agile education values
- Agile education roles
- Agile education meetings
- Agile education artefacts
- Agile education sample selection criteria during the screening process
- Self-directed morning checklists for students before going to school
- Exercise - agile learning

Objectives

After studying this unit, you should be able to:
- Understand Agile SCRUM Kanban concept in your personal life as parents or students and how to apply field rules for faster performance & better results
- Understand the tricky tips & traps of Agile, Scrum, KANBAN, etc.

Agile can empower students and parents. It's my opinion based on various international research works; it may vary from person to person(s).

3.1 Agile Learning vs. Traditional Learning

The key element of building Agility is a mindset. To understand the type of mindset shift expected from different stakeholders/people, the following table can be useful:

Element	Traditional learning	Agile learning
Syllabus	Limited, freeze, during course execution no or a little change without discussing with students.	Always open for relevant amendment to incorporate student-oriented pragmatic approach, interests, and performance.
Schedule and Timing	Followed the Waterfall approach. Very specific. Very difficult to allocate additional time if needed.	Divided into different blocks/units following being Agile mindset and education resilience.
Roles	Teachers – Source of knowledge and mainly passing one-way micro-managed communication to students. Students – Mainly passively absorb knowledge	Teachers – Interactively grooming students based on two-way communication using case studies, lesson learnt, game, brainstorming sessions etc., as applicable. Students – Always actively absorb knowledge. They are self-organized and active learners using the inspect, adapt, check, improve, and sustain principles.
Communication and interaction	Closed-ended.	Open-ended discussion on syllabus, progress, and educational institution(s).
Education theory and learning design	Based on behavior theory and teachers-oriented approach.	Based on constructive/adaptive/resilience theory and team-oriented analytical pragmatic collaborative learning.
Class structure	Highly hierarchical and mainly individual learning.	Flat hierarchy having provision of both group and individual learning.
Evaluation	Annual evaluation of students' performance based on marks.	Continuous evaluation of students' performance based on grades.

Table 3.1: Agile learning vs. traditional learning

Your description may vary, depending on what part of the principle stands out most for you, but the above-mentioned are possible abbreviations.

3.2 Agile Education Manifesto

Let's look at some key pointers of the "Agile Education Manifesto":

- Students and career guide/coach over administration and infrastructure

- Collaboration, empathy, proficiency, and active meaningful practical learning over theoretical learning, competition, & process compliance
- Pragmatic networking, sharing, and grade over syllabus and marks
- Wisdom and strategic continuous learning skills over aptitude and degree certificate

Alternatively, it may be articulated as:

- Teachers and students over administration and infrastructure
- Competence and collaboration over compliance and competition
- Employability and marketability over syllabus and marks
- Attitude and learning skills over aptitude and degree

Visit the following URL for details:

Source: - **https://files.eric.ed.gov/fulltext/EJ1157450.pdf**

3.3 Agile Education Principles

Let's look at some key pointers on "Agile Education Principles":

- Coping with uncertainty
- Working creatively and continuous pursuit of innovation
- Interactive two-way dialog during home work/school assignments/game/meetings/workshops with stakeholders
- Collaborative pragmatic approach of continuous learning
- Self-organized quick learners
- Face-to-face interactive conversation & brainstorming
- Critical and analytical thinking, enabling independent, skillful, happy individuals
- Self-motivation and motivating/grooming others
- Planning and implementation
- Interdisciplinary work fostering multidisciplinary team(s) formation
- Accountable self- motivated teams with controlled/optimized emotions and concerns
- Retrospectives at regular intervals following systemic thinking approach

We've said that agile is a mindset, not a specific set of practices, and many agile teams end up tailoring their agile methodology to their own circumstances.

Agile Education

Let's depict some key pointers of "Agile Education":

Figure 3.1: *Agile Education (Image Source – www.pmcolumn.com)*

We've said that agile is a mindset, not a specific set of practices, and many agile teams end up tailoring their agile methodology to their own circumstances.

3.4 Agile Education Values

Let's look at some key pointers on "Agile Education Values":

- Focus
- Openness
- Respect
- Courage
- Commitment

Your description may vary, depending on what part of the principle stands out most for you, but the above-mentioned are possible abbreviations.

3.5 Agile Education Roles

Generally, three roles are present:

- Students (like, SCRUM Team)
- Career guide/coach/teacher (like, SCRUM master)
- Principal (like product owner)

Your description may vary, depending on what part of the principle stands out most for you, but the above-mentioned are possible abbreviations.

3.6 Agile Education Meetings

Generally, four meetings are present:

- Bi-monthly principal, teachers & students meeting (like, Sprint planning)
- Daily students stand-up (like, daily SCRUM)
- Bi-monthly students progress assessment meeting (like, Sprint review)
- Bi-monthly Parents Teachers Meeting (PTM) (like, Sprint retrospective)

Your description may vary, depending on what part of the principle stands out most for you, but the above-mentioned are possible abbreviations.

3.7 Agile Education Artefacts

Generally, three artifacts are present:

- Bi-monthly task board (like, product backlog)
- Daily task board (like, Sprint backlog)
- Study books, study notes or students' progression/grade card (like, product increment)

The measures we used to see if the Minimum Viable Product (MVP) delivered achieved our expected market targets were:

1. A happier and much less stressed out child
   - Measured by attitude
   - General health and appearance
2. Improvement in academic metrics
   - Higher grades

- Better retention of learning objectives
- Nicer emails from her teachers that no longer had implied concerns about my parenting abilities

Outcome – Happy parents, happy students, independent skilful individuals.

Your description may vary, depending on what part of the principle stands out most for you, but the above-mentioned are possible abbreviations.

3.8 Agile Education Sample Selection Criteria During the Screening Process

Let's look at some key pointers on "Agile Education sample selection criteria during the screening process." The key element of building Agility is a mindset. To understand the type of mindset shift expected from different stakeholders, the following table can be useful:

Element	Selection criteria
Agile methodologies	• Agile applied in the classroom context • Agile used to manage projects selection and in group assignments • Agile used to define the syllabus • Agile used to organize workshops/ sessions
Pragmatic interactive learning	Evidence of instances delivered by means of Agile
Education effectiveness data points	Evidence of agile education competencies delivered by means of Agile application(s)
Education level	All levels with special emphasis on professional/higher education
Location	Worldwide
Language	Local native language PLUS English
Paper length	A4
Subject area	All subject areas

Table 3.2: Agile Education sample selection criteria during screening process

Your description may vary, depending on what part of the principle stands out most for you, but the above-mentioned are possible abbreviations. We've said that agile is a mindset, not a specific set of practices, and many agile teams end up tailoring their agile methodology to their own circumstances.

3.9 Self-directed Morning Checklists for Students Before Going to School

Let's look at some key pointers on "Self-directed morning checklists for students before going to school":

- Drink water or milk
- Take vitamins or medicine, if any
- Brush your teeth
- Eat breakfast
- Washroom (toilet, potty etc.)
- Shower or take bath
- Do morning chores/responsibility
- Backpack, shoes, and socks
- Update information boards

Your description may vary, depending on what part of the principle stands out most for you, but the above-mentioned are possible abbreviations.

Sample Task Board Showing 2 Swim Lanes

Let's depict some example(s) of "Sample task board showing 2 swim lanes":

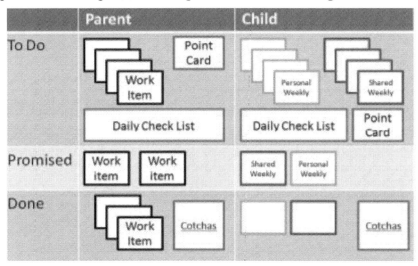

Figure 3.2: *Sample task board showing two swim lanes*

A Daily Task List

Let's depict some example(s) of "daily task list":

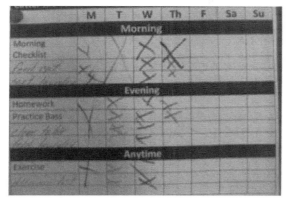

Figure 3.3: A daily task list

Parents/family Task Boards

Let's depict some example(s) of "Parents/family task boards":

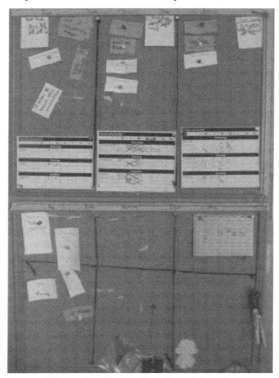

Figure 3.4: Parents/family task boards

3.10 Exercise - Agile Learning

Let's take up some review exercise:

- Use Agile concept to build this house:

Figure 3.5: Building

 o Need to be completed by March 2021

 o 170 floors need to be present

 o 103 elevators need to be present

 o 2 acres of land is present

Culture follows values, and practices follow culture. Values must always lead. A value is something people think helps them become better/transparent.

- Use Agile concept in students' lego games/building block games
- Use Agile concept in students' exam preparations
- Use Agile concept in students' job interviews preparations
- Use Agile concept in students' home work/school assignments
- Use Agile concept during pregnancy
- Use Agile concept in students' nursing

Conclusion

In this chapter, we mainly discussed:

- Agile learning vs. traditional learning
- Agile education manifesto
- Agile education principles
- Agile education values
- Agile education roles
- Agile education meetings
- Agile education artefacts
- Agile education sample selection criteria during the screening process
- Self-directed morning checklists for students before going to school

Parents, students, Scrum masters, product owners, developers, and professionals closely associated with Agile Scrum, Kanban, and XP projects can further improve their knowledge of Agile with valuable pragmatic insights. Entry-level professionals and Agile enthusiasts with relevant experience can also acquire in-depth knowledge of the concepts discussed in the Agile methodology tutorial.

In the next chapter, you should be able to:

- Cover real-life Agile Scrum KANBAN job interview questions and answers
- Understand the concept(s) of Agile, Scrum, Kanban
- Apply Agile, Scrum, and Kanban in your organization/project(s)
- Explore numerous tips & tricks to gain new customers by adopting and implementing Agile SCRUM Kanban in organizations/projects/programs and field rules for faster performance and better results
- Understand field rules for faster performance and better results
- Understand the critical success factors of adopting Agile over the Waterfall model

Let's go over some review questions.

Questions

1. **As Scrum Master, you read online that a competitor is about to release a new electronics product that offers the same innovative functionality the development team is working on. What should you do?**

   a. Tell the product owner to immediately reprioritize the backlog

   b. Do some research to determine whether the team's product will still have a unique angle

   c. Ask the product owner if this news changes the viability of the project

   d. Cancel the project

   e. Both a and b

2. **Which question is the concern of the project sponsor on team focus?**

    a. Does the team understand the technical requirements?

    b. Does the product owner understand the product well?

    c. Will the team deliver the expected value on time?

    d. Is the Scrum master prioritizing the features accurately?

    e. Both a and d

3. **As a member of an agile delivery team, what might you be working on?**

    a. Developing the project mission statement

    b. Determining which features are the most important

    c. Testing the product increment to see if it's working

    d. Deciding whether the product increment is acceptable

    e. Both b and d

4. **What will your agile team spend the least time focusing on?**

    a. Reflecting on their progress and how to improve their processes

    b. Improving performance by identifying the weakest links on the team

    c. Responding to new information that comes up while doing the work

    d. Learning through trial and error how to improve efficiency

    e. Both a and d

5. **Who does the below task(s)?**

    - Writes acceptance tests for the product increments
    - Holds daily scrum meetings
    - Regularly updates information radiators to share the team's progress with stakeholders

    a. Development team

    b. Scrum master

    c. Product owner

    d. Manager

    e. Testing lead

6. **The development team should focus on the following activities. Identify the odd ones:**

    a. Perform Sprint execution

    b. Inspect and adapt

    c. Groom the product backlog

    d.   Manage economics

    e.   Formulate techniques for effective product backlog management

7. **What should an agile team focus on?**

    a.   Knowing why agile is the best approach

    b.   Understanding why agile practices work

    c.   Documenting their agile roles and practices

    d.   Measuring their performance

    e.   Both c and d

8. **Development team should focus on the following SCRUM values. Identify the odd ones:**

    a.   Openness

    b.   Autonomy

    c.   Respect

    d.   Courage

    e.   Commitment

9. **How would you recommend that a team transitions to using agile?**

    a.   Identify a successful agile team and copy what they are doing

    b.   Learn what agile is trying to accomplish before deciding which practices to adopt

    c.   Hire the best Scrum master you can afford and make that person accountable for the transition

    d.   Try out some agile practices first to see if they are helpful in your situation

    e.   Both a and c

10. **What is most important for your agile development team to continuously focus on?**

    a.   Getting the right answers

    b.   Understanding their tasks

    c.   Defining their tasks

    d.   Assigning their tasks

    e.   Doing accurate estimation

Question Number	Answer	Explanation
1	c	**Correct Answer(s):** c. In four of these answer options, the Scrum master is stepping out of their role on an agile team. It isn't up to the Scrum master to analyze the value of the project, tell the product owner what to do, or especially, cancel the project. The only person mentioned here who can assess whether the project viability has changed is the product owner, probably in consultation with the project sponsor. So, the correct answer is to ask the product owner if the viability of the project has changed.
2	c	**Correct Answer(s):** c. The sponsor is responsible for ensuring that the project will deliver the expected value on time and on budget. They leave the technical requirements to the team and feature prioritization to the product owner, not the Scrum master. It is the product owner who communicates the product features to the team.
3	c	**Correct Answer(s):** c. The only good option here is testing the product increment to see if it's working. Other options are not being primarily taken care of by the agile development team. Thus, the other options are incorrect.
4	b	**Correct Answer(s):** b. All of these choices are aspects of the agile mindset as expressed in the Agile Manifesto, except identifying the weaker performers on the team. Agile teams improve their performance collaboratively, rather than by critiquing the performance of individual team members. That wouldn't be aligned with the principles of supporting and trusting the team to get the work done (principle 5).
5	a	**Correct Answer(s):** a. Manager and testing lead are not Agile Scrum roles. Scrum master or product owner never do the articulated tasks as these are being taken care of by the development team.
6	c, d, e	**Correct Answer(s):** c, d, e. Product owner primarily does the following activities: • Groom the product backlog • Manage economics Scrum master does the following activity: Formulating techniques for effective product bcklog management

7	b	**Correct Answer(s):** b. Agile teams should focus on understanding why Agile practices work. While they might feel that agile is the best approach for them, another approach might be better for another team or another scenario; Agile isn't "best" across the board for every team. While documenting roles and practices and measuring performance are done on an agile project, they aren't a key focus of the team.
8	b	**Correct Answer(s):** b. Scrum recognizes five fundamental values: focus, courage, openness, commitment, and respect. Autonomy is not a SCRUM value.
9	b	**Correct Answer(s):** b. We need to understand and integrate the mindset behind agile practices before we can use them effectively. So, the best way to transition to agile is to learn what agile is trying to accomplish and then use that understanding to guide which agile practices to adopt in our situation.
10	b	**Correct Answer(s):** b. Although all these activities are performed on an agile project, notice that the question asks what the team should "continuously focus on." This is a clue that the question is looking at the team's high-level process, not specific parts of their work. So, "Understanding their tasks" is most important for your agile development team to continuously focus on. Thus, the other options are incorrect.

CHAPTER 4
Interview Questions and Answers on Agile SCRUM KANBAN

Introduction

In this chapter, we will mainly discuss the following topics. After completing this lesson, you will be able to describe/explain/implement:

- Real-life Agile Scrum KANBAN job interviews questions and answers

- Understand the concept(s) of Agile, Scrum, Kanban

- Apply Agile, Scrum, Kanban in your organization/project(s)

- Numerous tips & tricks to gain new customers by adopting and implementing Agile SCRUM Kanban in organizations/projects/programs and field rules for faster performance & better results

- Understand field rules for faster performance and better results

- Understand critical success factors of adopting Agile over the Waterfall model

Certified Agile practitioners are in high demand. Organizations seeking to adopt a more agile method or SAP S/4 HANA now choose XP technical best practices, along with Scrum or KANBAN as their framework. So, a large part of the team's success depends on skilled professionals. It is on their hands to make a difference in the dynamics and performance of an agile team. Whether you are new to Agile or already an expert, it is always beneficial to know how to prepare for a job interview in this field.

Are you studying day and night but are still nervous? How can you crack the job interviews?

This artefact uncovers the different areas under which questions are asked and the most commonly asked ones. We hope these will help you while preparing for your job interview. The examples given in this artefact are user-focused and have been highly updated, including strategies, best practices, and real-life examples.

In this chapter, you should be able to understand/implement:

- Real-life Agile Scrum KANBAN Job interviews questions and answers
- The concept(s) of Agile, Scrum, Kanban
- Apply Agile, Scrum, Kanban in your organization/project(s)
- Numerous tips & tricks to gain new customers by adopting and implementing Agile SCRUM Kanban in organizations/projects/programs and field rules for faster performance & better results
- Understand field rules for faster performance and better results
- Understand critical success factors of adopting Agile over the Waterfall model

Happy learning!

Structure

In this chapter, we will discuss:

- Real-life Agile Scrum KANBAN Job interviews questions and answers

Objectives

After studying this unit, you should be able to:

- Understand the concept(s) of Agile, Scrum, Kanban
- Apply Agile, Scrum, Kanban in your organization/project(s)
- Numerous tips & tricks to gain new customers by adopting and implementing Agile SCRUM Kanban in organizations/projects/programs and field rules for faster performance & better results
- Understand field rules for faster performance and better results
- Understand critical success factors of adopting Agile over the Waterfall model

Happy learning!

1. **What are the critical success factors for an Agile SAP team?**

   Answer:

   Let's look at some key pointers on it:

   - Establish buy-in to the process at all levels
   - Establish confidence and proactively start with win-win situation and do something that can deliver a quick win
   - The art of storytelling
   - Do not be discouraged at the moment of first awkward use
   - Integrating members of team that are not co-located
   - Ability to remove impediments
   - Manage the flow of work
   - Establish a process and framework that works best with your culture, resources, and environment
   - Continuously update process and framework – learn and adjust

   Your description may vary, depending on what part of the principle stands out most for you, but the above-mentioned are possible abbreviations. We've said that agile is a mindset, not a specific set of practices, and many agile teams end up tailoring their agile methodology to their own circumstances.

2. **For any Agile project/program/portfolio in the backlog, who prioritizes the user stories?**

   Answer: Product owner

3. **For delivering Agile projects/program/portfolio, what activities are most critical?**

   Answer: These are:

   - Sprint planning
   - Release planning

4. **Explain valuable key lessons learned while Applying Agile to projects?**

   Answer: Let's look at some key pointers on it:

   - Be proactive in creating a model that works for the organizational culture
   - Be proactive in selecting the right first project, as not all projects are good candidates for Agile
   - Varying steps of adoption need to be considered
   - Find the Agile Champion

- Train the team at all levels
- Develop a willing to work product council
- Find the right product owner
- Focus more on team work rather than mechanics
- Collaboration over co-location
- Build effectively the backlog – story mapping and stories
- Set rules to make productive optimum team engagement
- Selecting the proper metrics and the proper reporting tools
- Process validated Lean Agile processes are incremental, iterative, and adaptive:
  - o Team was not disrupted by the scope changes
  - o Team generally made change adoption in just 3-4 sprints
- Key project / program stakeholders
  - o Confirm empirical evidence is better that Progress Reports
  - o Give proper slack time to teams and allow proper time in Scrum planning events to focus on "Value Add" work
  - o Team becomes "Being Agile" mindset and "Lean Thinkers" rather than just "doing Agile"
  - o Work products completed significantly ahead of stipulated Project milestone time

Your description may vary, depending on what part of the principle stands out most for you, but the above-mentioned are possible abbreviations. We've said that agile is a mindset, not a specific set of practices, and many agile teams end up tailoring their agile methodology to their own circumstances.

5. **How can users address the common impediments while applying Agile to ERP projects?**

   Answer: Let's look at some key pointers on it:
   - Assessing Agile readiness
   - Tailor the approach to the adoption lifecycle
   - Identify the case for change
   - Identify a champion for Agile
   - Change in roles and responsibilities
   - Select the right first project-demonstrate success
   - Set realistic expectations of delivery
   - Build a GREAT backlog

- Integrate organizational change management

Your description may vary, depending on what part of the principle stands out most for you, but the above-mentioned are possible abbreviations. We've said that agile is a mindset, not a specific set of practices, and many agile teams end up tailoring their agile methodology to their own circumstances.

6. **What is the count of minimum number of quality gates recommended in activate for any Agile project/program/portfolio?**

   Answer: Let's cover some key pointers on it. The following diagram explains SAP Activate Quality Gates:

Figure 4.1: SAP Activate Quality Gates (Image source – SAP AG / SE)

Your description may vary, depending on what part of the principle stands out most for you, but the above are possible abbreviations. We've said that agile is a mindset, not a specific set of practices, and many agile teams end up tailoring their agile methodology to their own circumstances.

7. **Explain the purpose of SCRUM of SCRUMs.**

   Answer: Scrum of Scrums focuses on integration topics and cohesive solution build. It consists of the development team and product owners from individual scrum teams.

Like daily scrums, scrum of scrums meetings take place on a regular schedule, but they are not necessarily daily. Let's say the individual teams have their daily scrum meeting at 9:00 a.m. After those meetings, at 9:30—perhaps daily or twice a week, as needed—someone from each team will take part in the scrum of scums meeting. If a participant learns about any issues that impact their team, they will report them to the rest of the team after the meeting.

Larger endeavors may even warrant a "scrum of scrum of scrums" where the teams repeat this pattern with a third-level meeting. Here, a representative from each scrum of scrums will attend a "scrum of scrum of scrums" to coordinate the work across a larger set of teams.

8. **In SAP Activate, mention the three pillars names for any Agile project/ program/portfolio?**

   Answer: These are:

   - SAP best practices
   - Guided configuration
   - Methodology

9. **Cut-over rehearsal completion is being done in which phase of the SAP Activate methodology for any Agile project/program/portfolio?**

   Answer: Deploy

10. **In SAP Activate, the blueprint phase is replaced by which phase for any Agile project/program/portfolio?**

    Answer: VALIDATE SOLUTION

    Validate to best practices with fit/gap workshops, capture delta.

11. **To estimate the relative size of the backlog, what technique can a project team use for any Agile project/program/portfolio?**

    Answer: Planning Poker

    Planning Poker® is a consensus-based estimating technique. Agile teams around the world use it to estimate their product backlogs. It can be used with story points, ideal days, or any other estimating unit.

12. **For New Implementation Cloud name, what is the last process flow step of the realization phase for any Agile project/program/portfolio?**

    Answer: Transition to operations to production support plan.

13. **In the Roadmap Viewer, name the most granular view for any Agile project/program/portfolio?**

    Answer: Deliverables and/or accelerators

14. **How can you address the common road blockers while Applying Agile to ERP projects for any Agile project/program/portfolio?**

    Answer: Let's look at some key pointers on it:

    - Assessing Agile readiness
    - Tailor the approach to the adoption lifecycle
    - Identify the case for change
    - Identify a champion for Agile
    - Change in roles and responsibilities
    - Select the right first project -demonstrate success
    - Set realistic expectations of delivery
    - Build a GREAT backlog
    - Integrate organizational change management

    Your description may vary, depending on what part of the principle stands out most for you, but the above-mentioned are possible abbreviations.

15. **Explain the common road blockers while Applying Agile to ERP projects for any Agile project/program/portfolio?**

    Answer: Let's look at some key pointers on it:

    - A new way to manage projects:
        o Makes all the dysfunction in a team or organization visible
        o Bad products will be delivered sooner with poor First Time Right Product quality and will cause faster failure for doomed projects
        o People may follow the mechanics without following the values of Agile
    - People are most comfortable with what they know
        o ERP project team members have an attachment to Waterfall development
        o Lack of talent recognition mechanisms (like, award, incentives) for increasing delivery speed
    - ERP configuration is NOT programming
    - Management of development objects integrated with Sprint delivery
    - Integrating off-shore development
    - Lack/poor sequencing of user stories, tasks, and activities and poor management of dependencies
    - Encompassing & integrated ERP solutions
        o Integrated end-to-end business processes are difficult to decompose

16. **What are some key lessons learned while Applying Agile to ERP projects for any Agile project/program/portfolio?**

    Answer: Let's go over some key pointers on it:

    - Keeping an Agile mindset rather than going Agile is key for business value addition
        - o Be proactive in creating a model that works for the organizational culture
    - Consider the various steps of adoption
    - Find the Agile Champion
    - Be proactive in selecting the right first project, not all projects are good candidates for Agile
    - Train the team at all levels
    - Develop a willing to work product council
    - Find the right product owner
    - Focus more on team work rather than mechanics
    - Collaboration over co-location
    - Build the backlog effectively – story mapping and stories
    - Set rules to make productive optimum team engagement
    - Select the proper metrics and the proper reporting tools
    - Process validated Lean Agile processes are incremental, iterative, and adaptive
        - o Team was not disrupted by the scope changes
        - o Team generally made change adoption in just 3-4 sprints
    - Key project/program stakeholders
        - o Confirm empirical evidence is better that progress reports
        - o Give proper slack time to teams and allow proper time in Scrum planning events to focus on "Value Add" work
        - o Team becomes "Being Agile" mindset and "Lean Thinkers" rather than just "doing Agile"
        - o Work products completed significantly ahead of stipulated Project milestone time

17. **What tools are there to support guided configuration source for any Agile project/program/portfolio?**

    Answer: Let's see some key pointers on it:

    - Solution Builder
    - Self-Service UIs

- Expert Configuration

18. **What are the key characteristics (6) of activate for any Agile project/ program/ portfolio?**

    Answer: Let's look at some key pointers:
    - START WITH BEST PRACTICES
      - o   Use ready-to run business processes
    - VALIDATE SOLUTION
      - o   Validate to best practices with fit/gap workshops, capture delta
    - MODULAR, SCALABLE AND AGILE
      - o   Structure project to deliver the solution incrementally
    - CLOUD READY
      - o   Leverage the flexibility and speed of the cloud
    - PREMIUM ENGAGEMENT READY
      - o   Build and Run fully supported via SAP control centers
    - QUALITY BUILT-IN
      - o   Identify risk early with total quality approach

19. **What are the deliverables for customer team enablement for any Agile project/program/portfolio?**

    Answer: Let's look at some key pointers on it:
    - Self-enablement
    - Customer team learning plan
    - Knowledge transfer

20. **What view is available under Phase in Roadmap Viewer for any Agile project/program/portfolio?**

    Answer: Let's go over some key pointers on it:
    - Phase
    - Work-stream
    - Deliverable

21. **What are the activities/deliverables in the preparation phase for New Cloud implementation for any Agile project/program/portfolio?**

    Answer: Let's go over some key pointers on it:
    - Customer team self-enablement
    - Project initiation and governance

- Project plans, schedule and budget
- Project standards and infrastructure
- Project kick-off and on-boarding
- Phase closure

22. **When does the project team formally hear the communication that the product owner approved the prioritized backlog for any Agile project/ program/portfolio?**

    Answer: Backlog is a living document, and the priorities of the stories could be updated regularly. Upon completion of the deliverable, "Design for Gaps and Deltas" in the EXPLORE Phase of Solution Design comes before Release and Sprint Planning.

23. **What phase is the handover to support task for any Agile project/program/ portfolio?**

    Answer: The Deploy phase

24. **What flow diagram depicts the SAP activate methodology new implementation and system conversion for any Agile project/program/ portfolio?**

    Answer: Let's depict some key pointers on it:

    - SAP Activate:

      SAP Activate New Implementation

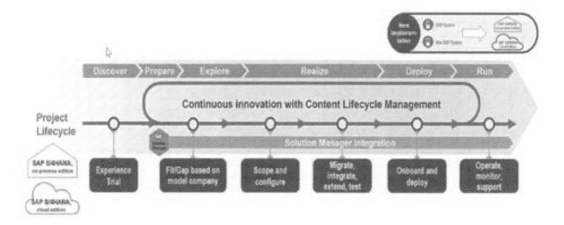

Figure 4.2: SAP Activate New Implementation (Image source – SAP AG / SE)

System conversion:

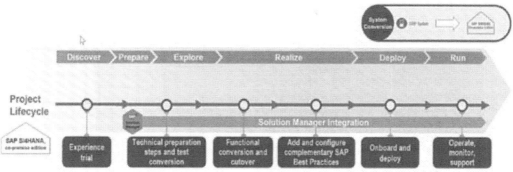

Figure 4.3: SAP Activate System Conversion (Image source – SAP AG / SE)

Your description may vary, depending on what part of the principle stands out most for you, but the above-mentioned are possible abbreviations. We've said that agile is a mindset, not a specific set of practices, and many agile teams end up tailoring their agile methodology to their own circumstances.

25. **What are the phases of the methodology for any Agile project/program/ portfolio?**

Answer: We've worked to bring in the simplicity of cloud implementation while retaining the content required for on-premise projects. We've struck a balance using these four phases:

- **Prepare:** The project is initiated and planned, including quality and risk plans. The system environment is set up, including best practices for ready-to-run processes.

- **Explore:** The customer team explores SAP solution capabilities, while the system integrator researches the customer's business. Together, they use fit/gap workshops to identify the configuration and extensions that best meet customer requirements.

- **Realize:** The team configures and extends the system based on prioritized requirements captured in the Explore phase. Configuration and build are done in short cycles, ensuring regular validation and feedback from the business. Structured testing and data migration activities ensure quality.

- **Deploy:** Final preparations before cutover to production ensure that that the system, users, and data are ready for transition to productive use. The transition to operations includes setting up and launching support and then handing off operations to the organization managing the environment.

Note:

- **Discover:** What resources are available before an SAP S/4HANA project starts
- **Prepare:** Infrastructure is set up and selected SAP Best Practices are activated
- **Explore:** Workshops define the solution and use SAP Best Practice processes
- **Realize:** Implementation is undertaken tracking all work in SAP Solution Manager
- **Deploy:** SAP Solution Manager is used in the production cutover
- **Run:** SAP Solution Manager is used to monitor and optimize the solution

Your description may vary, depending on what part of the principle stands out most for you, but the above-mentioned are possible abbreviations. We've said that agile is a mindset, not a specific set of practices, and many agile teams end up tailoring their agile methodology to their own circumstances.

26. **How do Agile and Lean act as a good combination for any Agile project/ program/portfolio?**

    Answer: Where Agile focuses on the delivery of software and systems, lean focuses on the optimization of the entire business operation. In organizations that use lean methods, all operating processes are tuned to each other to the maximum. Unnecessary procedures, bottlenecks, and other obstacles are removed where possible to facilitate an optimum 'flow'. It plays an important role for lean success. Just like lean, Agile is based on the premise that the people on the work floor are the best people to say how their work can be done better. The flexibility of Agile forms an excellent basis for a lean operating organization, just as speed, flexibility, and focus on customer value.

27. **What are the main benefits of Agile implementation in SAP Project for any Agile project/program/portfolio?**

    Answer: Let's look at some key pointers on it:

    - **Faster results**
        - o Iterative and incremental way of delivery of shippable products features based on customer priority in 1-4 weeks duration sprints
        - o CAST score from product owner/customer feedback after each sprint
    - **Increased flexibility**

- o Can respond to changes per 'sprint'
- o Use of relevant extreme programming and Devops best practices, like Continuous build, deployment, integration, test driven development, pair programming, and refactoring during software products delivery
- o Continuous communication, collaboration, and integration with business from day 1
- **More transparency**
  - o Monthly metrics data trend analysis
  - o Sprint reviews for checking the results and requirements
  - o Risks are quickly identified and, therefore, manageable
  - o Daily stand-up meetings for the DEV team
  - o Continuous communication, collaboration, and integration with business from day 1

Your description may vary, depending on what part of the principle stands out most for you, but the above-mentioned are possible abbreviations. We've said that agile is a mindset, not a specific set of practices, and many agile teams end up tailoring their agile methodology to their own circumstances.

28. **Explain the SAP Activate Methodology Principles for any Agile project/ program/portfolio?**

    Answer: Let's look at some key pointers on it:

    - **START WITH BEST PRACTICES** – Make effective use of ready-to-run business processes
    - **CLOUD READY -** Utilize the speed and flexibility of the cloud
    - **VALIDATE SOLUTION -** With fit-gap workshops, capture delta, and validate best practices
    - **PREMIUM ENGAGEMENT READY -** Via SAP control centers build and run fully-supported features
    - **MODULAR, SCALABLE AND AGILE** – Plan/prioritize project to deliver the end-to-end solution incrementally
    - **QUALITY BUILT-IN -** Identify risk early with total quality approach

    Your description may vary, depending on what part of the principle stands out most for you, but the above-mentioned are possible abbreviations. We've said that agile is a mindset, not a specific set of practices, and many agile teams end up tailoring their agile methodology to their own circumstances.

29. **What are SAP Activate building blocks for any Agile project/program/ portfolio?**

   Answer: Let's depict some important pointers about it.

   SAP Activate Building blocks:

SAP Activate building blocks

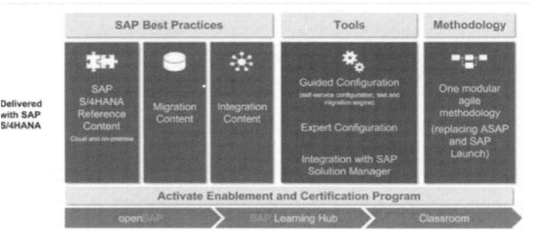

Figure 4.4: SAP Activate Building Blocks (image source – SAP AG / SE)

Your description may vary, depending on what part of the principle stands out most for you, but the above are possible abbreviations. We've said that agile is a mindset, not a specific set of practices, and many agile teams end up tailoring their agile methodology to their own circumstances.

30. **Explain one DEMO of Agile implementation in SAP Project for any Agile project/program/portfolio?**

   Answer: Let's depict some important pointers on it.

SAP activate implementation:

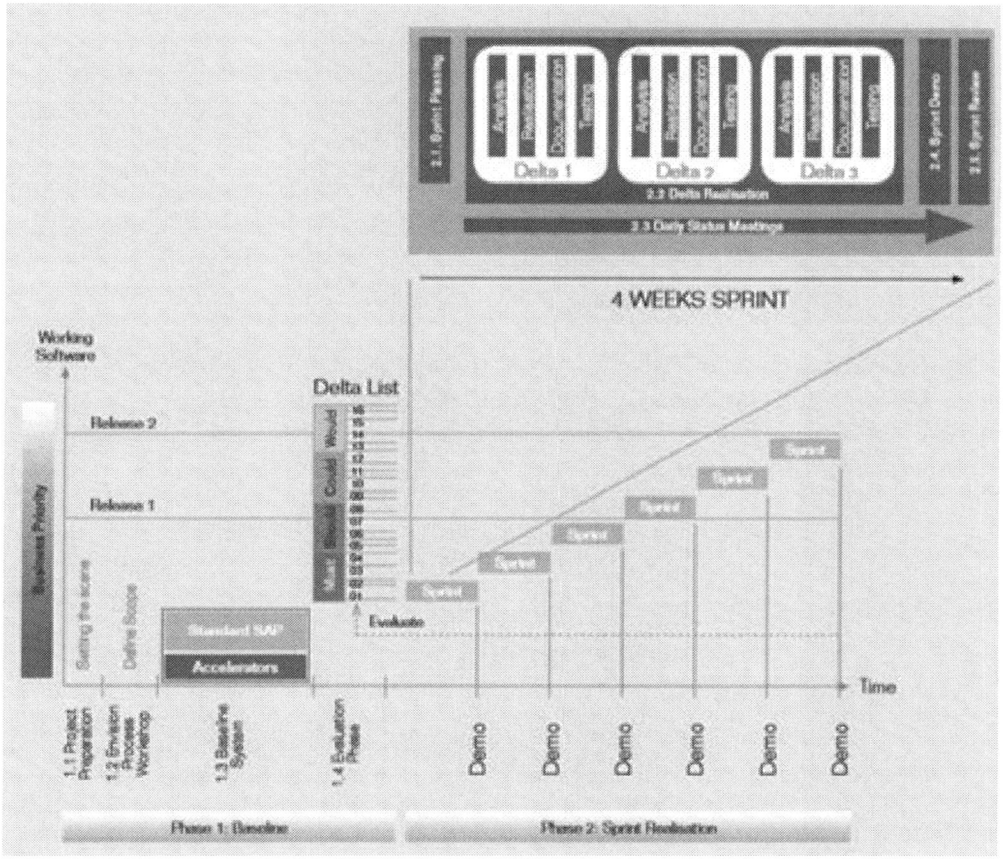

Figure 4.5: *SAP Activate implementation (Image source – SAP AG / SE)*

Your description may vary, depending on what part of the principle stands out most for you, but the above-mentioned are possible abbreviations. We've said that agile is a mindset, not a specific set of practices, and many agile teams end up tailoring their agile methodology to their own circumstances.

31. **When does the team complete the System Assessment in AP Activate Methodology for any Agile project/program/portfolio?**

    Answer: Prepare

32. **When does the DEV team receive formal feedback from the product owner for any Agile project/program/portfolio?**

    Answer: There is no formal meeting to get feedback from the product owner. Sprint review is an event to review the progress with the stakeholders. The PO should have seen the stories as they were completed and given feedback.

33. **To access the SAP Activate Methodology content in the Roadmap Viewer, which navigation option do you use for any Agile project/program/ portfolio?**

    Answer: Navigate by work stream

34. **In the Explore Phase during the Scope Validation/Fit-Gap Analysis activity, which accelerations can you use for any Agile project/program/portfolio?**

    Answer: Let's see some key pointers on it:
    - RICEF Specification Template
    - Solution Validation Workshop

35. **Name the component of SAP Activate that offers customers a reference solution in the cloud for a quick start for any Agile project/program/ portfolio.**

    Answer: SAP Best Practices

36. **In SAP Activate Methodology, name the key characteristics of the implementation approach for any Agile project/program/portfolio.**

    Answer: Let's see some key pointers on it:
    - Premium engagement ready
    - Validate solution
    - Start with SAP best practices

37. **What is the main purpose of a sprint retrospective meeting for any Agile project/program/portfolio?**

    Answer: Improve the SCRUM process

38. **How you can utilize the "Innovate" option of SAP Cloud Platform for your SAP S/4HANA Agile project?**

    Answer: Let's see some key pointers on it:

    To support innovation:
    - Use SAP Cloud Platform to create minimum viable products and proof-of-concept apps for your business quickly. Connecting these *"playground"* accounts to the systems with test data will help convince the business more than anything else.
    - Combine the platform's mobile services and SAP Leonardo Services with third-party data and services from our partner ecosystem to create new apps quickly.

    Your description may vary, depending on what part of the principle stands out most for you, but the above-mentioned are possible abbreviations. We've said that agile is a mindset, not a specific set of practices, and many agile teams end up tailoring their agile methodology to their own circumstances.

39. **When does the team identify and design functional quick wins in scope of the conversion project in SAP Activate methodology for any Agile project/program/portfolio?**

    Answer: Explore

40. **What are the currently available SAP S/4HANA deployment options for any Agile project/program/portfolio?**

    Answer: SAP currently plans to offer on-premise, cloud (public and managed), and hybrid deployments.

41. **What is the purpose of Fit/Gap analysis for an Agile S/4 HANA Project?**

    Answer: The primary objective is to have an updated and approved Scope Baseline to move into the Realization phase:

    • Validate pre-activated or pre-assembled solution in Sandbox system

    • Drive towards adopting SAP standard processes

    • Ensure that SAP implementation meets customers' business needs

    • Discover, clarify, and negotiate solution design

    • Identify and capture delta business requirements and gaps (on top of the initial Sandbox system)

    • Prioritize delta requirements and gaps

    • Prevent the need for rework during realization

42. **Give example of "Project Governance - In an Agile context"?**

    Answer: Let's depict some important pointers on it:

    Project governance in Agile context

    Leveraging its experience gained over various engagements and industry best practices, Delivery Partner is proposing the following well-structured governance model to ensure effective project-level governance and delivery. The three-tier governance structure will define, delegate, monitor, and guide all aspects of the engagement and focus on the following dimensions:

    • Periodic performance review

    • Risk and issue management at appropriate level

    • Escalation management

    • Ensuring management support to the engagement

This project management structure is based on the following three levels:

Strategic level

The strategic level consists of steering committee:

- To provide strategic direction to the project
- Ensures that the project is aligned to the strategic vision of customer/ business
- Creates business value and is aligned to its IT strategy

Tactical level

The tactical level comprises the evaluation team, which will ensure that the multiple work-streams in the project:

- Follow the overall agreed program timelines
- Provide the right interface for all the work-streams to manage inter-dependencies
- Follow standardized processes like release management and change management
- Follow the design and utilize common knowledge repository

Operational level

This level consists of the IT and User teams, which will ensure daily operational management of the project.

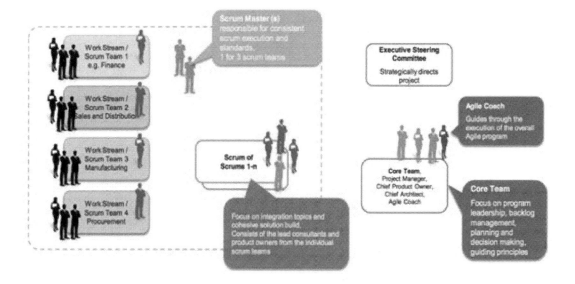

Figure 4.6: Project governance in Agile context (Image source – SAP AG / SE)

Your description may vary, depending on what part of the principle stands out most for you, but the above-mentioned are possible abbreviations. We've said that agile is a mindset, not a specific set of practices, and many agile teams end up tailoring their agile methodology to their own circumstances.

43. **Give an example of SAP Agile team structures.**

    Answer: Let's depict some important pointers on it:

    SAP Agile team:

* Regular cadence of meetings between SCRUM Masters of all SCRUM teams

* Goal is to coordinate and align work; highlight dependencies; discuss cross-topics

* SCRUM Masters have responsibility to debrief their respective teams on the results

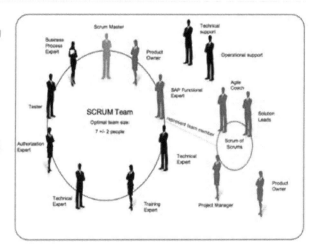

Figure 4.7: SAP Agile team

Your description may vary, depending on what part of the principle stands out most for you, but the above are possible abbreviations. We've said that agile is a mindset, not a specific set of practices, and many agile teams end up tailoring their agile methodology for their own circumstances.

44. **What is Scrum?**

    Answer: Scrum is an agile way to manage a project, usually software development. Agile software development with Scrum is often perceived as a methodology; but rather than viewing Scrum as methodology, think of it as a framework for managing a process. – Mountain Goat. It emphasizes teamwork, communication, and speed across complex projects. The Scrum master is the one who manages how information is exchanged.

    Scrum is a process framework for new product development created by Jeff Sutherland and KEN SCHWABER. The word "Scrum" is taken from the Rugby game, where the team huddle is called Scrum. Since new product development is complex, Scrum offers an iterative and incremental development approach. There are three roles in Scrum, namely, Scrum master, product owner and development team of size 3-9. All three roles are empowered to do their job and have no authority on each other, but they work as self-organizing team to deliver a product with complimenting skills.

Scrum is an empirical process used for solving complex problems like software development. Since we cannot predict the outcome upfront, the team goes iteratively and learns and improves each time. For the team to continuously learn and improve, they keep all the artefacts transparent and frequently inspect and adapt.

45. Why would I need a Scrum Master certification?

Answer: A Scrum Master certification demonstrates the core knowledge of the Scrum process. It is an added advantage as it proves the holder as a continuous learner. It shows ambition, which boosts professional growth. Here are a few benefits of getting a Scrum certification:

- It provides with Scrum principles and skills
- It prevents challenges and obstacles that may occur while using an Agile platform
- It enhances team collaboration
- It brings a change of mindset for the whole team
- With the growing demand for Scrum masters, holding a certification adds a competitive advantage and builds a stronger professional credibility.

46. Who is a Scrum master?

Answer: The Scrum master is responsible for supporting and promoting the Scrum. They assist their team in meeting their goals. They help managing project risks and mentor the team as its coach. The Scrum master is also known as a servant leader, as they provide collaboration and motivate the team to deliver their best.

Scrum master is a Scrum process champion who teaches, coaches, and mentors the product owner and the development team so that they can deliver a product in Scrum process. Their main responsibility is to remove any impediments that the PO and development team are facing so that they can deliver high-value and high-quality products.

47. What is a "user story" in Scrum?

Answer: A user story is a tool used in Agile software development that captures the description of a feature from an end-user perspective. It describes, among others, the type of user and their motivations. A user story creates a simplified description of a user's requirements.

The purpose of a user story:

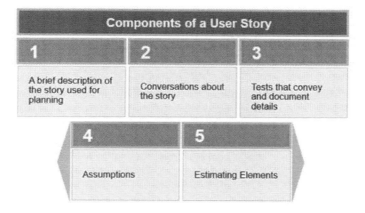

Figure 4.8: The purpose of a user story

A user story describes functionality that will be useful to a stakeholder of the system. User stories – example:

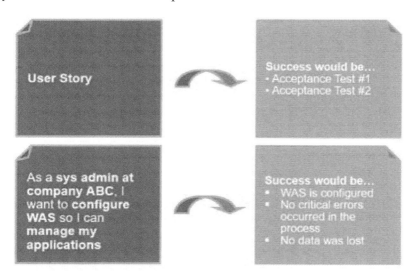

Figure 4.9: User stories: An example

Your description may vary, depending on what part of the principle stands out most for you, but the above-mentioned are possible abbreviations.

48. **What are the three main artifacts of the Scrum process?**

Answer: Let's see some key pointers on it:

- Product backlog

- Sprint backlog
- Product increment

We've said that agile is a mindset, not a specific set of practices, and many agile teams end up tailoring their agile methodology to their own circumstances.

49. What do you understand by the term Scrum Sprint? What is its duration?

Answer: A Scrum Sprint is a repeatable cycle during which the work is completed and made ready for review. The duration of the Scrum Sprint depends on the size of the project and the team working on it. Generally, it is under 30 days.

50. Describe the role of a product owner.

Answer: The product owner focuses on the success of the product, ensuring its business value. Their main responsibility is to identify and refine the product backlog items.

The Product Owner (PO) collaborates with customers (users) of the product being developed and understands their needs to create a list of customer needs in a product backlog and always keep it in the order of business value. This way, the PO ensures that the latest needs of the customer are delivered by the development team. The PO is also responsible for effective product backlog management and helping the development team build the high-value product and perform long-term planning and tracking. The product owner is responsible for the product's success.

51. How does the Scrum master help the product owner?

Answer: Let's see some key pointers on it:

- Efficient product backlog management
- Helping the Scrum team in adopting a shared vision
- Understanding and practicing agility
- Facilitating Scrum events as requested or needed

Your description may vary, depending on what part of the principle stands out most for you, but the above are possible abbreviations.

52. How does the Scrum master serve the organization?

Answer: Let's see some key pointers on it:

- Helping in Scrum adoption.
- Acting as an Agile change agent.
- Helping the team and increasing productivity.
- Ensuring the iterative incremental cycle of continuous improvement. The dot voting technique is often used for this.

- Supporting Agile leadership principles, leading to organizational transformation.

We've said that agile is a mindset, not a specific set of practices, and many agile teams end up tailoring their agile methodology to their own circumstances.

53. **Why is the Agile methodology necessary?**

   Answer: Let's see some key pointers on it:
   - It helps achieve customer satisfaction with the rapid delivery of useful software
   - It eases potential changing requirements, even late in a company's development
   - Repeatedly delivers working software, the main measurement of progress
   - It provides close, daily cooperation between the company and the developers
   - Having self-organizing teams brings self-motivated team members
   - In situations of co-location, it assists communication through face-to-face conversations
   - It offers continuous attention to XP
   - It adds simplicity

   Your description may vary, depending on what part of the principle stands out most for you, but the above-mentioned are possible abbreviations.

54. **Explain Scrum overview.**

   Answer: Let's see some key pointers on it:
   - Scrum is a processed framework meant to help teams develop projects in an iterative, incremental manner. The process is organized in cycles of work called Sprints.
   - These cycles do not last more than 4 weeks each (usually 2 weeks), and they are timeboxed, which means they end on a specific date regardless of whether the work has been completed. They are never extended.
   - At the beginning of each Sprint, the team chooses one of the project's tasks from a prioritized list. They agree on a common goal of what they believe they can deliver at the completion of the Sprint, something that is tangible and realistic. No additional tasks should be added during the Sprint.
   - The team meets every day to review their progress and adjust the steps needed to complete the remaining work.

- At the end of the Sprint, the team reviews the work cycle with the stakeholders and shows the end product. With the feedback they get, they plan the next Sprint.

- Scrum emphasizes obtaining a working product at the completion of each Sprint. When talking about software, this means a system that is integrated, tested, end-user documented, and shippable.

Let's depict some key pointers on it. SCRUM Process in a nutshell:

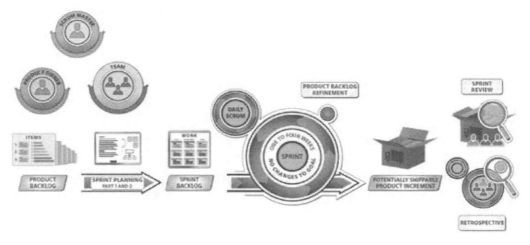

Figure 4.10: SCRUM Process in a nutshell (Image Source: https://www.scrumalliance.org)

Scrum is a process framework for new product development created by Jeff Sutherland and KEN SCHWABER. The word "Scrum" is taken from the Rugby game, wherein the team huddle is called Scrum. Since new product development is complex, Scrum offers an iterative and incremental development approach. Scrum has three roles, namely, Scrum master, product owner and the development team of size 3-9. All three roles are empowered to do their job and have no authority on each other. However, they work as self-organizing team to deliver a product with complimenting skills.

SCRUM process in a nutshell – Example:

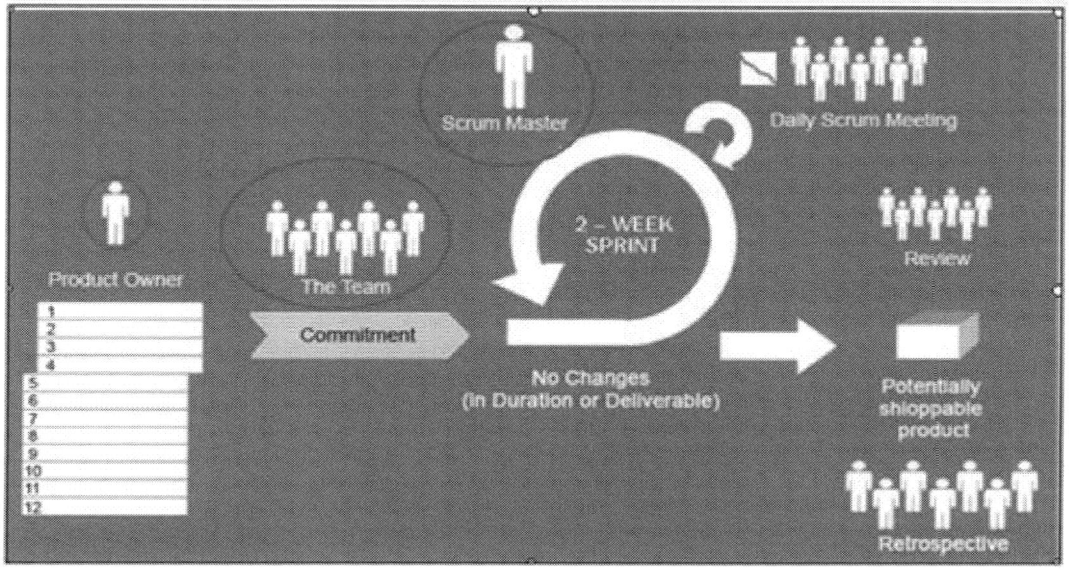

Figure 4.11: SCRUM in a nutshell (Image Source: https://www.scrumalliance.org)

Product is delivered in short iterations called Sprints, which range between 1 and 4 weeks. At the end of the Sprint, a small increment of the product is delivered to the customer. This increment should add value to the customer and should be of high quality, and the user should be able to use it if they decide to. So, product increment should be fully developed and tested and a usable addition to the product.

On the first day of the sprint, the development team and PO get together for a meeting called Sprint Planning to decide how much from product backlog should be taken into Sprint based on the development team's capacity and capability. This work is called Sprint backlog. Once the Sprint is planned, the development team works collaboratively every day. The team meets at least once a day for a 15-minute synch up called daily scrum to ensure that they are all on the same page. They identify any impediments that cause the Sprint goal to fail. Scrum master helps the team and PO resolve those impediments so that they go forward.

The goal for the team is to deliver a working product increment at the end of the sprint. Once the product increment is created, the PO invites a few stakeholders to review the product and give their feedback. The development team demonstrates what they have produced in the Sprint in a meeting called Sprint Review. Based on the feedback, the product will be adjusted if needed.

The development team and the PO meet to reflect on what went well and what could be better after the Sprint Review in a meeting called Sprint Retrospective to identify any improvement areas they can work on. The product owner and development team meet a few times every sprint to look at the product backlog to make it ready for the upcoming sprints. These activities are called Product Backlog Refinement. Since product backlog should be kept evolving to allow changes for the product, the product Backlog Refinement is an ongoing process to make the elaborate requirement just in time. Scrum master helps the product owner and development team by facilitating Scrum meetings effectively, coaching them on the Scrum values and process.

The success of Scrum implementation heavily depends on Scrum master's role. This is not an authoritative role. Scrum Master is like a servant leader who serves the team and helps them achieve the goals. For Scrum master to be effective, the role should be empowered, i.e., the Scrum master should be given full authority to implement the Scrum process. Other than understanding the Scrum framework in depth, Scrum master needs to acquire a few additional skills like facilitation, coaching, mentoring, and teaching to effectively guide the Scrum team.

55. **What are the five phases of risk management?**

    Answer: Let's see some key pointers:

    - Risk identification
    - Risk categorization
    - Risk response
    - Risk review
    - Risk closure

    We've said that agile is a mindset, not a specific set of practices, and many agile teams end up tailoring their agile methodology to their own circumstances.

56. **What are the main tools used in a Scrum project?**

    Answer: Let's see some key pointers:

    - JIRA
    - Rally
    - Version One
    - Azure

    Your description may vary, depending on what part of the principle stands out most for you, but the above-mentioned are possible abbreviations.

57. How can a Scrum master track the progress of a Sprint?

Answer: Scrum masters can track the Sprint progress using the Sprint burndown chart. The vertical axis shows the new estimate of work remaining, while the horizontal one shows the number of Sprints.

This graph shows a new estimate of how much work remains each day until the team is finished.

Tracking progress during Sprint – Example 1:

Product Backlog Item	Sprint Task	Volunteer	Initial Estimate of Effort	New Estimates of Effort Remaining at end of Day...					
				1	2	3	4	5	6
As a buyer, I want to place a book in a shopping cart	modify database	Sanjay	5	4	3	0	0	0	
	create webpage (UI)	Jing	3	3	3	2	0	0	
	create webpage (Javascript logic)	Tracy & Sam	2	2	2	2	1	0	
	write automated acceptance tests	Sarah	5	5	5	5	5	0	
	update buyer help webpage	Sanjay & Jing	3	3	3	3	3	0	
	. . .								
Improve transaction processing performance	merge DCP code and complete layer-level tests		5	5	5	5	5	5	
	complete machine order for pRank		3	3	8	8	8	8	
	change DCP and reader to use pRank http API		5	5	5	5	5	5	
. . .		. . .	. . .						
		Total	50	49	48	44	43	34	

Figure 4.12: Tracking progress during Sprint – Example 1 (Image Source: https://www.scrumalliance.org)

Typically, burndown charts show either the estimated time remaining, as shown here, or the estimated story points remaining. A story point is basically a unit of work that has been defined by the team.

Sprint burndown chart – Example 1:

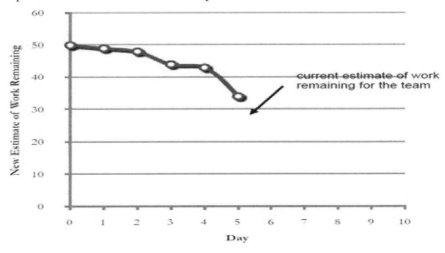

Figure 4.13: Sprint burndown chart – Example 1 (Image Source: https://www.scrumalliance.org)

We've seen that agile teams rely on low-tech, high-touch tools displayed on highly visible information radiators, and burn charts are one of the most common tools displayed in this way. Burn charts are important because they make the team's progress visible at a glance and make it easy to forecast when the project (or a release within the project) will be complete.

There are two kinds of burn charts: burndown and burnup. Burndown charts show the estimated effort remaining on the project, and burnup charts show the features that have been delivered already.

Tracking progress during Sprint – Example 2:

Task	Task Owner	Hours of Work Remaining on Each Day of the Sprint									
		Day 1	Day 2	Day 3	Day 4	Day 5	Day 6	Day 7	Day 8	Day 9	Day 10
Configure database and space IDs for Trac	Sanjay	4	4	3	1	0					
Use test data to tune the learning and action model	Jing	2	2	2	2	1					
Setup a cart server code to run as apache server	Philip	3	3	5	2	0					
Implement pre-Login Handler	Tracy	3	3	3	3	3					
Merge DCP code and complete layer-level tests	Jing	5	5	2	2	2					
Complete machine order for pRank	Jing	4	4	3	3	3					
Change DCP and reader to use pRank http API	Tracy	3	3	0	0	0					
Total		50	48	44	43	34					

Figure 4.14: Tracking progress during Sprint – Example 2 (Image Source: https://www.scrumalliance.org)

A burndown chart tracks the work that remains to be done on a project. As work is completed, the progress line on the chart will move downward, reflecting the smaller amount of work that still needs to be done. The most common use of burndown charts is for measuring the team's progress in completing the project work.

Sprint burndown Chart – Example 2:

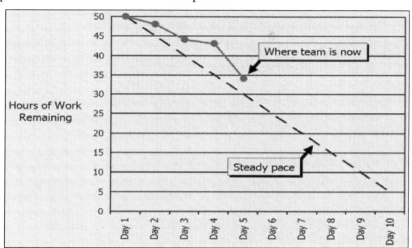

Figure 4.15: Sprint burndown chart – Example 2 (Image Source: https://www.scrumalliance.org)

58.   What is timeboxing in Scrum?

Answer: Timeboxing means allotting a fixed unit of time for an activity. The unit of time is called a time box. Sprint is also timeboxed to 2-4 weeks.

59.   Is cancelling a Sprint possible? Who can cancel a Sprint?

Answer: A Sprint can be cancelled before the Sprint timebox limit ends. Only the product owner can cancel the sprint.

60.   How is estimation in a Scrum project done? What are the techniques used for estimation?

Answer: Estimation in a Scrum project is done using relative Agile estimation techniques:

- The T-shirt estimation technique
- The planning poker estimation technique
- The estimation by analogy technique
- The disaggregation estimation technique

We've said that agile is a mindset, not a specific set of practices, and many agile teams end up tailoring their agile methodology to their own circumstances.

61.   What are the roles involved in the Scrum framework?

Answer: A Scrum framework has three roles:

- Scrum master
- Product owner

- Development team

62. **What is the difference between change management in a Waterfall and in Agile Scrum?**

    Answer: In Waterfall, change management is based on the change management plan, the change tracker, and the release plan based on which the consultants deliver their work. In agile, there is no change management plan. Based on the definition of ready product backlog, team is grooming Sprint backlog and delivering their work.

63. **What is the purpose of a daily Scrum?**

    Answer: The daily Scrum meeting is for the team. It helps them self-organize toward their sprint commitment and set the context for the next day's work.

    Daily SCRUM meeting:

Who attends?	The development team's participation is mandatory. Product owner or SCRUM master's participation is optional, but they can attend it based on the request.
When happens?	Every day of the Sprint. **Choose a time that works for everyone.** It is held at the same time and place every day to reduce complexity.
Time-box	Maximum length of 15 minutes or less.
Input	Sprint Goal and Sprint Backlog
Outcome	Plan for next 24 hours and list of impediments (if any).
General questions discussed	During the meeting, each team member explains: • What they did yesterday that helped the team meet the Sprint Goal. • What they will do today to help the team meet the Sprint Goal. • Do they see any impediments that prevent them or the team from meeting the Sprint Goal? In a nutshell, it's interactive bilateral communication to understand: • Where the development team is in terms of achieving the Sprint Goal? • What can the development team do differently, i.e., how the team can change tactics to achieve more towards the Sprint Goal to produce releasable product increment? • Development team tracks sprint roadmap progress based on Sprint burndown/burnup charts where Effort **Unit Story Points** is plotted against Sprint number of day.

Generic challenges	- The team is all working on separate things, no common Sprint Goal. - 'Mini-waterfall' syndrome i.e., cross-dependency. - Self-organization is a buzz word that has little practical meaning for the team. - All teams are not in sync in case of distributed teams. - Mobile Friendly Cloud enabled cost optimum tool is missing for 24/7/365 customer support. - JIRA Tool has many limitations.
Daily Scrum meeting best practices	• Choose a time that works for everyone. • Always focus on outcome rather than output. • Always focus on achieving the Sprint Goal. • Keep stand-up efficient and keep everyone engaged, avoid making duplicate conversation, and make the discussion short and crispy. Rotate who keeps time to ensure that everyone is accountable and invested. If everything is fine, you may make it less than 15 minutes. **Remember that it's a problem identification meeting, not a problem solving meeting.** • Stand in a circle near your desks • Review and update sprint backlog every day • No side conversations • Meeting rules notice • Same time and same place every day Make effective use of **Daily Scrum Meeting (DSM) Tool**, JIRA Tool, Stride + stand-up for distributed teams. **DSM)** APPLICATION SOLVES MANY PRACTICAL ISSUES THAT EVERY PROJECT EXPERIENCES IN THE DEVELOPMENT STAGE. Manage your workload, communicate with your team, and celebrate success.
Benefits of daily Scrum meeting	• Improves communication within the team. • Identifies impediments, if any, to facilitate early removal of the same so as to minimize impact on the Sprint. • Highlights and promote quick decision-making. • Improves the team's level of knowledge.
Tools/ techniques used	DSM Tool , JIRA Tool, Stride + stand-up for distributed teams. Telemetry technique is used to measure value. Dot Voting and Bottom-Up facilitation techniques are used for decision making.
Summary	Update and coordination by continuous inspection and adaptation of the sprint backlog; **it's a planning event, not status tracking event.**

Table 4.1: Daily SCRUM meeting

64. What do you understand by the term scope creep? How do you prevent it from happening?

Answer: If the requirements are not properly defined at the start and new features are added to the product already being built, a scope creep occurs. To prevent it:

- The requirements must be clearly specified
- The project progress must be monitored
- Effective grooming of sprint backlog must be done

65. What are the most common risks in a Scrum project?

Answer: Let's see some key pointers:

- A scope creep
- Timeline issues
- Budget issues

We've said that agile is a mindset, not a specific set of practices, and many agile teams end up tailoring their agile methodology for their own circumstances.

66. What do you understand by Minimum Viable Product in Scrum?

Answer: A Minimum Viable Product (MVP) is a product with the minimum required features to be shown to the stakeholders and be eligible to ship for production.

67. What is the major advantage of using Scrum?

Answer: Early feedback as well as the production of the Minimal Viable Product to the stakeholders would be the main advantages of using it.

68. What does DoD mean? How can this be achieved?

Answer: Definition of Done (DoD) is formed by a list of tasks that define the work's quality. It is used to decide whether an activity from the Sprint backlog is completed.

General

- Create the feature branch and push the changes according to above recommendations
- Code produced (all 'to do' items in code completed)
- Code commented, checked in and run against the current version in source control
- Peer reviewed (or produced with pair programming) and meeting development standards
- Builds without errors - check Sonar

- Unit tests written and passing
- Deployed to system test environment and passed system tests
- Passed User Acceptance Testing (UAT) and signed off as meeting requirements
- Any build/deployment/configuration changes implemented/documented/communicated
- Relevant documentation/diagrams produced and/or updated
- Remaining hours for task set to zero and task closed

AEM

- Component names are the same in the codebase and in the dialog
- TOUCHUI dialog is defined for the component
- Component lifecycle (add component, edit dialog, activate for publish) is tested:
  - o Default-values are implemented where necessary and tested
  - o Component is tested in the targeted browsers
  - o Changing component properties should not break the current and other components
- Sonar test passed by Java code
- Test coverage level is covered
- Component/feature has been tested on publish instance (with a dispatcher)
- Sample content for the component has been added
- Clients for the component has been updated with CSS and JS files

Definition of Done – Example 1:

Let's depict some example(s) on "Definition of Done":

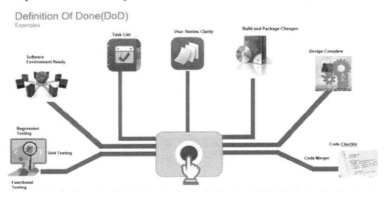

Figure 4.16: *Definition of Done – Example 1 (Image Source: https://www.scrumalliance.org)*

Sample Definition of Done:

- Code produced (all 'to do' items in code completed)
- Code commented, checked in and run against the current version in source control
- Peer reviewed (or produced with pair programming) and meeting development standards
- Builds without errors
- Unit tests written and passing
- Deployed to system test environment and passed system tests
- Passed User Acceptance Testing (UAT) and signed off as meeting requirements
- Any build/deployment/configuration changes are implemented/documented/communicated
- Relevant documentation/diagrams produced and/or updated
- Remaining hours for task set to zero and task closed.

Definition of Done – Example 2:

Let's depict some example(s) on "Definition of Done":

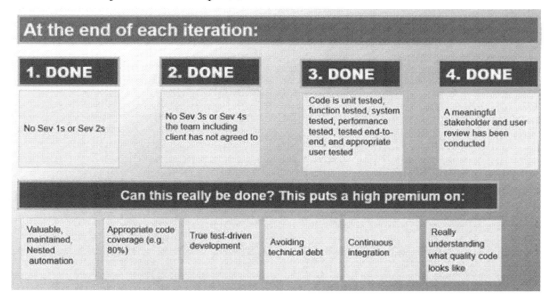

Figure 4.17: Definition of Done – Example 2

We've said that agile is a mindset, not a specific set of practices, and many agile teams end up tailoring their agile methodology to their own circumstances.

69. **What is velocity in Scrum?**

   Answer: Velocity calculates the total effort the team has put into a Sprint. The number is obtained by adding all the story points from the previous Sprint. It is a guideline for the team to understand the number of stories they can do in a Sprint.

70. **List out the disadvantages of Scrum.**

   Answer: Let's see some key pointers on it:

   • Daily Scrum meetings require frequent reviews and substantial resources

   • A successful project relies on the maturity and dedication of the whole team

   • The uncertainty of the product, the changes, and frequent product delivery remain present during the Scrum cycle

   • It depends on a significant change

   Your description may vary, depending on what part of the principle stands out most for you, but the above-mentioned are possible abbreviations. We've said that agile is a mindset, not a specific set of practices, and many agile teams end up tailoring their agile methodology to their own circumstances.

71. **Explain Scrum phases and processes.**

   Answer: Let's see some key pointers on it. SCRUM phases and processes in a nutshell:

Scrum Phases and Processes

Initiate	Plan & Estimate	Implement	Review & Retrospect	Release
Create Project Vision	Create User Stories	Create Deliverables	Demonstrate and Validate Sprint	Ship Deliverables
Identify Scrum Master & Stakeholder(s)	Estimate User Stories	Conduct Daily Standup	Retrospect Sprint	Retrospect Project
Form Scrum Team	Commit User Stories	Groom Prioritized Product Backlog		
Develop Epics	Identify Tasks			
Create Prioritized Product Backlog	Estimate Tasks			
Conduct Release Planning	Create Sprint Backlog			

Figure 4.18: SCRUM *phases and processes in a nutshell (Image Source: https://www.scrumalliance.org)*

Your description may vary, depending on what part of the principle stands out most for you, but the above-mentioned are possible abbreviations.

72. What's SCRUM Flow?

Answer: SCRUM process flow in a nutshell:

Scrum Flow

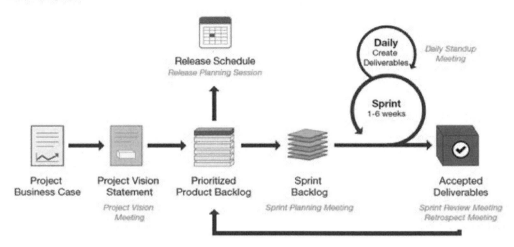

Figure 4.19: SCRUM process flow in a nutshell (Image Source: https://www.scrumalliance.org)

73. What's Definition of Ready?

Answer: Meeting a Definition of Ready means that stories must be immediately actionable. Here's a sample Definition of Ready:

- User Story is clear
- User Story is testable
- User Story is feasible
- User Story defined
- User Story acceptance criteria defined
- User Story dependencies identified
- User Story sized by development team
- Scrum team accepts user experience artefacts
- Performance criteria identified, where appropriate
- Scalability criteria identified, where appropriate
- Security criteria identified, where appropriate
- Person who will accept the User Story is identified

Team has a good idea what it will mean to demo the User Story.

74. **What's the PDCA Cycle in SCRUM?**

Answer: PDCA cycle in SCRUM

Let's depict some important pointers on it. It's just like Deming PDCA cycle like plan, do/execute, check/take feedback, and act/improve & sustain:

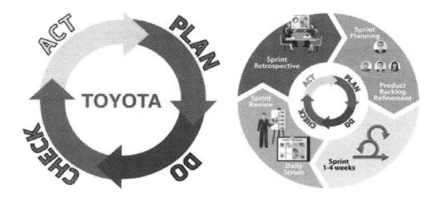

Figure 4.20: PDCA cycle in SCRUM (Image Source: https://www.scrumalliance.org)

We've said that agile is a mindset, not a specific set of practices, and many agile teams end up tailoring their agile methodology to their own circumstances.

75. **Why SCRUM Master is a Servant Leader?**

Answer: SCRUM Master is system thinker. They have more value to:
- Empathy
- Active listening
- Persuasion
- Conflict resolution
- Effective questioning skills
- Protecting team members from outside odds and impediments removal
- Self-awareness
- Continuous learning
- Credibility

We've said that agile is a mindset, not a specific set of practices, and many agile teams end up tailoring their agile methodology to their own circumstances.

76. **What factor decides to do project in SCRUM way?**

Answer: When in complex environment we have specified timebox and definition of ready in the product backlog for our development work, i.e., we can use SCRUM where the volume of work is predictable.

77. **How can SCRUM handle real-life issue?**

    Answer: Suppose, two SCRUM team members take sick leave tomorrow. You are supposed to give delivery after two weeks and are following waterfall methodology. What you should do? All other team members are very busy and primary (P1) and secondary resource (P2) concept is not there.

    We will check from the resource whether anybody is doing any low-priority work where the delivery date is later. We will ask them to keep aside the low-priority work and do high-priority work.

78. **What did you do as SCRUM master to prevent scope creep?**

    Answer: Although the framework itself reduces the scope creep, I performed scope management to control the changes effectively.

79. **Give an example of a positive risk in your SCRUM project.**

    Answer: We are finishing the second sprint well ahead of the delivery schedule.

80. **Provide an example of a negative risk in your SCRUM project.**

    Answer: The product owner on the project is quitting the job even if his backup is not ready.

81. **What are the main reasons for crashing schedule in your SCRUM project?**

    Answer: To deliver products well ahead of the project milestone date.

82. **Can we use DevOps in your SAP scrum project?**

    Answer: Yes, by using ABAPGIT and Jenkins as per the latest update from SAP TechEd.

83. **Where are customers involved in SCRUM?**

    Answer: Customers are involved in sprint review and in sprint planning.

84. **What makes daily SCRUM a waste of time?**

    Answer: Let's see some key pointers on it:

    - The team members are doing multi-tasking and are not in sync with each other's work. They put more stress on individual performance and focus less on teamwork.
    - The team members are working on SCRUMBUT project. It is not 100% Scrum and not 100% waterfall.
    - The team members are geographically distributed in multiple countries. Each team member is unaware of the others' work and focus less on being a self-organized team.

We've said that agile is a mindset, not a specific set of practices, and many agile teams end up tailoring their agile methodology to their own circumstances.

85. What techniques are used in daily SCRUM?

Answer: Dot voting and bottom up facilitation techniques are used for decision making.

86. Who attends daily SCRUM?

Answer: Let's see some key pointers on it:

- The development team's participation is mandatory
- Product owner or scrum master's participation is optional

Your description may vary, depending on what part of the principle stands out most for you, but the above-mentioned are possible abbreviations.

87. What are the differences between product backlog and Sprint backlog?

Answer: Let's see some key pointers:

The key element of building Agility is a mindset. The following table can understand the type of mindset shift expected from different stakeholders:

Product backlog	Sprint backlog
The requirements	Individuals signs up for work of their own choice
A list of all desired work on the project	Estimated work remaining is updated daily
Ideally expressed such that each item has value to the users or customers of the product	Any team member can add, delete, and change the Sprint backlog
Prioritized by the product owner (MoSCoW rule)	If work is unclear, define a sprint backlog item with a larger amount of time and break it down later
Reprioritized at the start of each Sprint	Update work remaining as more becomes known

Table 4.2: Differences between Product backlog and Sprint backlog

Your description may vary, depending on what part of the principle stands out most for you, but the above-mentioned are possible abbreviations.

88. What's the MoSCoW Prioritization technique?

Answer: Let's see some key pointers on it:

The key element of building an Agility is a mindset. Here's a table to help understand the type of mindset shift expected from different stakeholders:

Letter	Stands for	Which means
M	Must have	• Minimum set of essential requirements, without which the system would be useless (MMF). • All of these requirements must be satisfied.
S	Should have	• Important requirements for which there is a short-term workaround. The system is useful without them. • These requirements can be included in the initial project scope but may be removed from the project scope to accommodate modified requirements.
C	Could have	• These requirements are valuable and nice-to-have but can easily be left out of the solution. • These requirements may be left out of the initial scope of the release to accommodate a time constraint.
W	Would have/ Won't have	• Time-permitting. • As changes to requirements or project progress dictates, lower priority requirements may be removed from the scope of the project.

Table 4.3: MoSCoW prioritization technique

We've said that agile is a mindset, not a specific set of practices, and many agile teams end up tailoring their agile methodology to their own circumstances.

89. **Where is following Agile not appropriate?**

Answer: Agile is not appropriate for:

- **PROJECTS** without significant complexity, urgency, and uniqueness.
- **TEAMS** that are not self-organizing and do not believe in inspecting and adapting.
- **ORGANIZATIONS** that do not invest in good XP practices (e.g. TDD, CI etc.) and cross-functional teams.
- **CUSTOMERS** who are not willing to be part of the product development team and provide continuous feedback.
- Big Bang – across the board changes without experimentation.
- Iterative development without automated tests.
- Sprints (Iterations) that deliver incomplete work.
- Doing mini-waterfalls within the Sprint (iterations).
- Implementing Agile without believing in its core values and principles.

- Projects where scope is almost frozen and doing upfront planning/ design.
- Projects just "DOING AGILE" rather than "BEING AGILE" mindset.
- Projects believing in doing all customer projects using 100% automation and following analogous estimation.
- Projects using PUSH principles rather than following PULL principles.

We've said that agile is a mindset, not a specific set of practices, and many agile teams end up tailoring their agile methodology to their own circumstances.

90. **On what parameters are Sprints empirical?**

    Answer: Sprints are empirical with regard to:

    - Outcomes (how valuable will this feature be?)
    - Outputs (how much can we get done?)
    - Approaches (how should we work?)

    Your description may vary, depending on what part of the principle stands out most for you, but the above-mentioned are possible abbreviations.

91. **Mention some major product owner anti-patterns.**

    Answer: Product owner anti-patterns. In pairs or small groups, discuss your experience with the following anti-patterns or speculate on the impact of:

    - Absent product owner - Product owner generally absent in Scrum ceremonies like Sprint Planning & Sprint Review
    - Product owner Scrum master - One person performs the role of both Scrum master and product owner
    - Token product owner
    - Penniless product owner

    We've said that agile is a mindset, not a specific set of practices, and many agile teams end up tailoring their agile methodology to their own circumstances.

92. **Mention the approach users need to follow to achieve the outcome of "Agile Manifesto Results Pyramid"?**

    Answer: The Agile Manifesto was created during a meeting in February 2001 that brought together a number of software and methodology experts who were in the forefront of the emerging agile methods. The people in attendance were:

    - KENT BECK
    - MIKE BEEDLE
    - ARIE VAN BENNEKUM

- ALISTAIR COCKBURN
- WARD CUNNINGHAM
- MARTIN FOWLER
- ROBERT C. MARTIN
- STEVE MELLOR
- KEN SCHWABER
- JEFF SUTHERLAND
- DAVE THOMAS
- JAMES GRENNING
- JIM HIGHSMITH
- ANDREW HUNT
- RON JEFFRIES
- JON KERN
- BRIAN MARICK

Agile Manifesto:

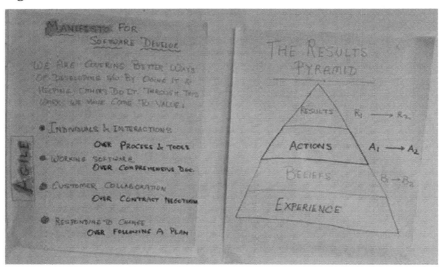

Figure 4.21: Agile Manifesto

Try to follow the bottom-up approach in "The Results Pyramid" to achieve the outcome.

93. **Explain Scrum Master tips on the dot voting technique.**

    Answer: Are you using dot voting? There is a major flaw in how dot voting *usually* gets facilitated. All votes need to be unbiased, but in reality, people placing the dots towards the end can get biased by dots already placed (and they can change their mind at the last minute by looking at the patterns). This approach is flawed. Have you seen this before? Or experienced it yourself as a participant?

It can be rectified by first having people WRITE DOWN their individual choices concurrently and privately, say, on post-it notes (so it is unbiased) and then place the votes by showing their written choices. Alternatively, the facilitator can call out individually asking for the participants' choices, they still show their post-its to the group. This way, dot voting will be more unbiased. This can be used for weighted dot voting as well (votes have unequal weights, and different colours correspond to different weights).

94. **Explain some useful tips for successful daily stand-up meetings.**

    Answer: Let's see some key pointers on it:
    - Identify the mistakes: It's not a status call. There should be a common shared vision on daily stand-up meetings among scrum teams.
    - Keep meetings short and simple with specified agenda.
    - Get your meetings off to the best possible start with prior relevant home works of team members on an index card about their work.
    - Don't be afraid to acknowledge constraints, use prompts to encourage them to speak up.
    - Make sure that attendance levels are high.
    - Make sure everyone is heard.
    - Don't be afraid to change things as relevant.

    We've said that agile is a mindset, not a specific set of practices, and many agile teams end up tailoring their agile methodology to their own circumstances.

95. **How can you work with difficult people?**

    Answer: Use interpersonal skills, conflict resolution skills, negotiation skills, and good effective questioning skills to deal with difficult people.

96. **What are the different coaching models currently available in the market?**

    Answer: Some of the currently available coaching models are mentioned here, but we need to know the context and which model we need to use when.
    - GROW
    - TGROW
    - OSKAR
    - OUTCOMES

- SPACE
- ACHIEVE
- POSITIVE

We've said that agile is a mindset, not a specific set of practices, and many agile teams end up tailoring their agile methodology to their own circumstances.

97. What are the coaching KATA questions for improvement?

Answer: Here are the five coaching KATA questions for improvement:

- What is the target condition?
- What is the actual condition now?
- What obstacles are preventing you from achieving the desired final condition?
- What is your next step (PDCA experiment)?
- Step back, learn, improve, sustain, and reuse. When can users go and inspect your lessons learnt at a particular step?

Your description may vary, depending on what part of the principle stands out most for you, but the above-mentioned are possible abbreviations.

98. What are the seven habits of a highly empathetic coach?

Answer: Here are the seven habits of a highly empathetic coach:

- Getting curious about strangers
- Active listening and being vulnerable
- Offering your support
- Practicing emotional detachment
- Being fully present when with people
- Following another person's life
- Asking better effective questions

We've said that agile is a mindset, not a specific set of practices, and many agile teams end up tailoring their agile methodology to their own circumstances.

99. What are the tips to coach for greatness?

Answer: Inspect, adapt, step back and give feedback, improve, and sustain.

100. What are the common characteristics of a self-organized team?

Answer: A self-organized team should have the following characteristics:

- They are autonomous
- They have a common purpose

- They learn from each other continuously
- They take ownership of their job/activity/task
- They share and care for each other's
- They are leader - leader on their own (shared leadership)

We've said that agile is a mindset, not a specific set of practices, and many agile teams end up tailoring their agile methodology to their own circumstances.

101. **What are the points to look at while building Agile culture?**

Answer: While building Agile culture, we need to look at eight points:

- Look for opportunities where you can appreciate others
- Help individuals where they can perform better and you can appreciate
- Share the common goal with the team members and share the expectations; help them set stretch goals
- Create an appreciation platform; make it shorter and frequent
- Create the 4 Cs mechanism between stakeholders: connect, collaborate, communicate, and celebrate

  Create many ways for appreciation, e.g., writing best code, sharing best stories, helping others in a crisis situation, best support team members, creative team members, blue thanks, kudos, pat on back etc.

- Celebrate the achievements
- Make it visual, on the board where all the team members can see; make it user-friendly and self-explanatory
- Recognize best ideas, best solutions, best knowledge shared, etc.

  Recognize the skills, knowledge, behaviours, and demeanour that support Lean agile performance to reinforce them at all levels of the organization. A culture of recognition engages, energizes, and empowers employees.

102. **What are the techniques to look at while building intuition?**

Answer: Mitchell and Stevens recommend these four techniques to help you build intuition:

- Meditate
- Do a blind reading
- Play red-light green-light
- Learn more through readings and classes

We've said that agile is a mindset, not a specific set of practices, and many agile teams end up tailoring their agile methodology to their own circumstances.

103.   How can we sustain a change initiative?

Answer: Some pointers are articulated here:

- Have a focus group with experts who can bring and effectively implement those changes smoothly
- Let's have a periodic review on the changes and improvements/outcomes achieved in the organization and communicate with all the stakeholders
- Connect with stakeholders, understand their concerns/pain areas, and collaborate
- Series of communication at different levels and get the feedback
- Use different ways to engage stakeholders to participate, and facilitate those events to connect with people
- Let us talk openly about stakeholders' voice and concern in a common area so that there is no secret mission
- Build win-win situations wherever possible
- Take the help from all the team members wherever possible, and resistance will slowly become cooperation

We need to keep looking and calibrate the situation to sustain the changes for long.

104.   What skills does the project manager need to unlearn in the Agile world?

Answer: Project Managers need to unlearn he following skills in the Agile world:

- Command and control mindset
- Plan driven mindset, upfront planning attitude for all things
- Less experimental mindset
- Less adaptability
- Highly process-focused mindset
- Outdated project and product development knowledge
- Discomfort with ambiguity

We've said that agile is a mindset, not a specific set of practices, and many agile teams end up tailoring their agile methodology to their own circumstances.

105.   What are the major challenges generally faced while creating Agile Centre of excellence (CoE)?

Answer: Some of the challenges could be:

- Less budget for CoE build and setup
- Insufficient competency

- Internal power conflicts
- Complaints from other business units
- Unable to provide customized "FIT-FOR-PURPOSE" solution at the right time as per business needs

We've said that agile is a mindset, not a specific set of practices, and many agile teams end up tailoring their agile methodology to their own circumstances.

106. **Name the different activities learning organizations are skilled in.**

Answer: Learning organizations are skilled in five main activities:

- Systematic problem solving
- Experimentation with new approaches
- Learning from their past experiences and lessons
- Learning from others' experiences and best practices
- Transferring the assets, lessons learnt, and best practices docs to the organization for reusability purposes

Your description may vary, depending on what part of the principle stands out most for you, but the above are possible abbreviations.

107. **What are the advantages of Scrum?**

Answer: Let's see some key pointers:

- Accelerate time to market
- Early and continuous customer validation
- Greater visibility into project progress
- Early defect detection and prevention
- Risk reduction and quality improvements
- Improve team morale

We've said that agile is a mindset, not a specific set of practices, and many agile teams end up tailoring their agile methodology to their own circumstances.

108. **What are the disadvantages of Scrum?**

Answer: Let's see some key pointers:

- It's hard!
- Makes all dysfunction visible
  - o Scrum doesn't fix anything, the team has to do it
  - o Feels like things are worse at the beginning
- Bad products will be delivered sooner, and doomed projects will fail faster

- High risk of turnover
    - o Some people will refuse to stay on a Scrum team
    - o Some people will refuse to stay if Scrum is abandoned
- Partial adoption may be worse than none at all
- If adoption fails, time will have been wasted, and some people may leave

Your description may vary, depending on what part of the principle stands out most for you, but the above-mentioned are possible abbreviations.

109. Name key enablers to improve coaching.

Answer: Some of the key enablers to improve coaching are articulated here (irrespective of any coaching model):

- Communicate shared common vision and clear expectations in team
- Build relationships
- Give feedback on areas that require specific improvement(s)
- Help remove impediments
- Listen actively
- Groom, give gentle advice and guidance
- Give emotional support, including empathy
- Reflect content or meaning
- Effective questioning techniques
- Gain commitment to change
- Applaud good results

Your description may vary, depending on what part of the principle stands out most for you, but the above-mentioned are possible abbreviations.

110. Mention the different surprising techniques used by an agile team to write better user stories in less time with less aggravation.

Answer: We've said that agile is a mindset, not a specific set of practices, and many agile teams end up tailoring their agile methodology to their own circumstances.

- Technique 1 - Have quarterly story-writing workshop with significant objective. Focus on one goal on MVP (Minimum Viable Product) and MMF (Minimum Marketable Product).
- Technique 2 - Master the art of splitting stories.
- Technique 3 - Add just enough detail, just in time.

111. **Mention the three qualities of potentially releasable or shippable product increment.**

Answer: The top three qualities of potentially releasable or shippable product increment are:

- High quality
- Properly tested
- What it does, it does well

Your description may vary, depending on what part of the principle stands out most for you, but the above-mentioned are possible abbreviations.

112. **What is the development team?**

Answer: The development team is cross-functional (all product development skills like development, testing, analysis, design etc. in the same team) and self-organizing (empowered to make decisions about how to build the product). It is responsible for delivering a quality product with the product owner's guidance.

113. **What are the reasons to take an Agile Certification?**

Answer: Agile is going to create 21st century's business model disruptions. So, it is important to choose the right agile certifications for your career growth. This adds some confusion to the young professionals, as they have stepped into Agile world recently.

It applies to freshers too. They are planning to build their career in Agile project management and remain concerned about which role should they choose to make their career in. In fact, they struggle to understand whether there is any difference in these roles? Also, why are they are named different if they are the same?

This article uncovers the differences between PMI-ACP® and SAFe® Agilist agile certifications. This is definitely a good article to read and understand the nuances of these roles. Who is a PMI Agile Certified Practitioner? What does a SAFe Agilist (SA) do?

We will start with the importance of these agile certifications need. This will lay the foundation for better clarity on the subject of discussion. Then, we will discuss the differences between these two agile certifications:

- Agile certified consultant can deliver project and product as per the end user's perspective.
- Agile certified consultant can deliver project and product in incremental & iterative way. They can adhere to extreme programming & lean principles (as applicable).

- Agile certified consultant can deliver project and product to maximize ROI. Agile certified consultant can maximize the stakeholders delight by gaining in-depth knowledge in Agile.

- Scrum / Agile certification is a must to deliver work with the best team velocity/productivity. Agile certified consultant can maintain good first-time right products quality. Here, the teams are self-organized and cross-functional.

Agile Manifesto illustration

Let's depict some important pointers:

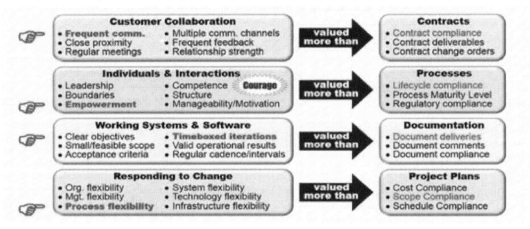

Figure 4.22: Agile Manifesto illustration (Image Source: https://www.scrumalliance.org)

- Agile Certification is a must to get more salary and promotion

- An Agile certified consultant can get different tips & traps in Agile project management. You can get different delivery management strategies and tips on customer-centric focus. It helps them create transparency at workplace via different Scrum ceremonies.

- Agile Certification helps a consultant stay aligned with the current industry trends. Agile Certification helps a consultant adhere to best practices.

- After agile certification, you can become Agile community member. Thus, you can enhance your skill sets by iteration with your peers. You can inspect and adapt through transparent continuous feedback loops.

- Agile certified consultant can act as a change agent and can drive organizational change.

- Agile certification helps a consultant improve their skill sets in different techniques, servant leadership.

- Agile training and certification helps a consultant facilitate stakeholder discussion and road mapping. It also helps them for product discovery.

- It helps them improve and manage the product backlog, product management. Agile certified consultants can also perform effective release planning.

- Agile certified consultants can effectively implement engineering practices, technical debt.

- The volume of work is sometimes unpredictable, and often, a bottleneck situation arises. Then, it is very tough for the consultant to handle it. But Agile certified consultant can manage the flow of work. They can do mapping between customer demand and supply.

- Agile certified consultant can manage project and product with good quality. Agile certified consultants can deliver projects as per signed SLA or KPIs. They can deliver products through incremental & iterative shippable products delivery. They can abide by Agile/scrum and Lean values, principles, and worldview.

- It helps them focus on quick response to the proposed changes. It comprises short duration iterations.

- Agile training and certification helps consultants in scaling organizational development and conflict resolution. It also helps consultants in Agile facilitation and coaching.

- Agile certified consultants can find creative ways to help organizations. They can help their peers adopt the Agile framework and capitalize on its benefits.

Be the change YOU want to see...Roll up your sleeves and show them how it's done.

- Mahatma Gandhi

Choosing a certification that is best for you doesn't lead to the success that you deserve. The effectiveness of the course depends on the training provider, so always choose the Agile certification based on your experience.

114. **What is PMI-ACP® certification?**

Answer: Project Management Institute (PMI) offers the Agile Certified Practitioner (ACP) certification. It is for professionals currently using agile or moving to agile practices. Team leads, project leads, or leadership professionals can attend this certification. It is also for Being Agile practitioners following daily agile principles and methodologies.

115. What are the benefits of PMI-ACP® certification?

Answer: Let's discuss some important pointers:

- Agile Certified Practitioner can apply Agile principles and values in different Agile methodologies like SCRUM, XP, Lean, KANBAN, and so on. So, it gives them better visibility.

- Better salary; the salary of a certified PMI ACP professional is about 28% higher than that a non-certified professional.

- Agile Certified Practitioner can perform as Change agent in continuous improvement initiatives. So, they can add values in their organization, which increases their credibility.

- Keeping up to current market trends.

- To manage the projects in an effective way as Being Agile.

- If your organization is looking forward to introduce Agile framework for achieving high-end project goals, the PMI ACP certification is the best choice.

- Agile Certified Practitioner can do Agile risk management.

- Agile Certified Practitioner can do Agile value stream analysis, value-based prioritization.

- Agile Certified Practitioner can do RCA using statistical methods like five WHYs and fishbone diagram analysis.

- Agile Certified Practitioner can plan and manage Agile KPIs.

- Agile Certified Practitioner can plan and manage Agile Metrics.

- Agile Certified Practitioner can follow and drive Agile Manifesto, principles, values, tools, techniques in projects.

Your description may vary, depending on what part of the principle stands out most for you, but the above-mentioned are possible abbreviations.

116. What is SAFe® Agilist?

Answer: A Certified SAFe® Agilist practitioner is a lean agile change agent in large IT organizations while working with multiple teams.

117. What are the benefits of SAFe® Agilist?

Answer: Let's see some key pointers:

- Better visibility, as a Certified SAFe® Agilist practitioner can apply Lean-Agile Mindset and principles.

- Better salary; the salary of a certified SAFe Agilist professional is about 30% higher than that a non-certified professional.

- Certified SAFe® Agilist practitioner can drive many value-added activities in an organization, so it increases their credibility.

- Keeping up to the current market trends.

- A Certified SAFe® Agilist practitioner can manage portfolios of agile teams and can do lean agile budgeting.

- A Certified SAFe® Agilist practitioner can plan and execute program increments.

    SAFe Agilist and Scaled Agilist terms are synonyms. This is the position given to a person who has completed the Leading SAFe course. The two-day information course and certification exam creates the following outcomes:

- Successful application in Agile enterprise environments.

- Recognition of the Lean-Agile mindset.

- Development and empowerment of consultants through Lean portfolio.

- Support of Agile leadership principles. It drives itself to organizational transformation.

- Continuous iterative incremental cycle of continuous improvement. You can use dot voting technique for this.

Your description may vary, depending on what part of the principle stands out most for you, but the above-mentioned are possible abbreviations.

118. PMI-ACP® vs. SAFe® Agilist : Name the key differentiators.

Answer: The key element of building an Agility is a mindset. This table can help understand the type of mindset shift expected from different stakeholders:

Sr. No.	Description	PMI-ACP®	SAFe® Agilist
1	Training	It requires 21 professional development units PMI ACP training. It can be classroom or online training from **Registered Education Provider (R.E.P.)**	It is mandatory to attend two days SAFe agile certification classroom training. The course covers SAFe defined content by training providers.
2	Certification course fee	- PMI ACP certification cost for online self learning is $400. - PMI ACP certification cost for live online training is Rs. 34930. Visit the site for detailed info about PMI ACP certification course. **PMI ACP certification provider URL –** **https://www.greycampus.com/pmi-acp-training-instructor-led**	Various worldwide vendors provide the SAFe agile training, and it costs around $1,000. Visit the site for detailed info about SAFe agile certification course. SAFe Agilist certification provider URL – **https://www.scaledagile.com/certification/which-course-is-right-for-me/**

3	Experience/ eligibility/ prerequisites	a. 2000 hours or 12 months of real-time project experience (earned in last five years) in managing project teams. b. Additionally, 1500 hours or 8 months of real-time Agile project experience (earned in the last 3 years) with agile methodologies. c. 21 hours of Agile training in agile methodologies, values, lean agile principles, practices, tools and techniques. d. Secondary degree (associate's degree or high school diploma or global equal).	a. 5+ years of experience in business analysis, testing, software development, project or product management. b. Experience in SAFe SCRUM. They ensure scrum team's adherence to Scrum during agile projects.
4	Exam cost	For PMI member, agile certified practitioner PMI ACP certification cost is $435.00 (Computer based exam fee). For Non PMI member, agile certified practitioner PMI ACP certification cost is $495.00 (computer-based exam fee). And paper-based exam fee is: - $385 for PMI member - $445 for Non PMI member	Safe agile certification cost is $995 per course. Here, the first exam attempt is free.
5	Course content	Agile project management training course table of contents include the following: - Many Agile methodologies like SCRUM, XP, Kanban, Lean - Agile Manifesto, principles, values, tools, techniques - Scrum artefacts, roles, ceremonies - Estimation techniques, Agile planning, monitoring and adapting - Agile risk management - Agile Metrics - Agile value stream analysis, value-based prioritization - Agile product quality - Communication - Interpersonal skills - Process improvements, Kaizen	SAFe certification training course table of contents includes the following: - Apply Lean-Agile Mindset and principles - Plan and execute program increments - Execute and release value through Agile Release Trains - Build an Agile portfolio with Lean-Agile budgeting - Apply DevOps principles - Apply SAFe principles for product owner - Apply SAFe principles for Scrum master

		- Statistical methods like five WHYs, fishbone diagram analysis - Agile Contracting - Agile Project chartering - Agile hybrid models - Managing with Agile KPIs **Agile Project Management certification exam** - 120 objective-type questions to answer in three hours duration	**SAFe agile certification exam** - 45 objective-type questions to answer in 90 minutes duration - Passing score is 34 out of 45, i.e., 75% is the SAFe certification passing score.
6	**Certification validity & renewal**	- Earn 30 **Professional Development Units (PDUs)** every 3 years. - Renewal of PMI ACP certification needs to be done every 3 years. - Renewal fee is $60.	You need to renew SAFe Agilist certification or scaled agile certification every year by paying a renewal fee of $100.
7	**Course accreditation**	**Project Management Institute (PMI)** offers it.	Scaled Agile offers it.
8	**Salary**	The salary of a certified PMI ACP professional is about 28% higher than that a non-certified professional.	The salary of a certified SAFe Agilist professional is about 30% higher than that a non-certified professional.

Table 4.4: Differences between PMI-ACP vs. SAFe Agilist

Your description may vary, depending on what part of the principle stands out most for you, but the above-mentioned are possible abbreviations.

119. **How can you determine which Agile Certification is a best fit for your career?**

Answer: It's three-step approach:

- Choose the Agile Certification that is the best fit for your career path and in line with your current job role & skill sets.

- We can correlate it in the following three-step approach to choose the best Agile certification as per your current career path.

Let's depict how to choose your Agile certification:

Figure 4.23: How to choose your Agile certification

Conclusion

Team leads, project leads, or leadership professionals can attend this certification. It is also for Being Agile practitioners following daily agile principles and methodologies. A PMI-ACP certified consultant helps your company achieve high-end project goals.

The PMI-ACP® Exam is not limited to the Scrum framework. It also includes other frameworks like Lean, Kanban, and XP. PMI-ACP® is an advanced examination compared to the basic Scrum Master certifications. You also need to take classroom or online training before appearing for the exam.

SAFe Agilist could be an ideal choice for you if you are working with multiple teams in the adoption of Scaled Agile Framework in your enterprise. SAFe Agilist and Scaled Agilist terms are synonyms. This is the position given to a person who has completed the **Leading SAFe** course.

Finally, it's imperative that a PMI Agile Certified Practitioner's role is more of a leadership role. While SAFe Agilist's duties include more of facilitating and coaching role, which certification to choose is entirely upon you. It should be in line with the capability you would like to grow in your professional life.

Choosing a certification that is best for you doesn't lead to the success you deserve. The effectiveness of course depends on the best training provider, so always choose based on your experience.

120. **What are some Scrum master certification exam sample questions?**

   Answer: You need to attend two days' workshop to get an idea of scrum master certification questions. Follow your CST class instructions strictly and read all the Scrum books.

121. **Is it difficult to crack a Scrum Master interview?**

   Answer: No. You need to have at least 2 years of hands-on scrum experience.

122. **What are the primary skills that a recruiter looks for?**

   Answer: Servant leadership

123. **What are the latest updates for interviewees?**

   Answer: You can get these from Agile scrum blogs.

124. **List some important tips to prepare for an interview.**

    Answer:

    • Review the most commonly asked questions, which are listed above.

    • Research and gather information about the company.

    • Find a way to develop a connection with the interviewer.

    • Be positive and confident.

    • End the interview on a positive note.

125. **Give an example of shared ownership of client/user outcomes by teams.**

    Answer: There's the idea that team members "hold themselves mutually accountable." In other words, the team has shared ownership for the project outcome.

    Here's an example of shared ownership:

    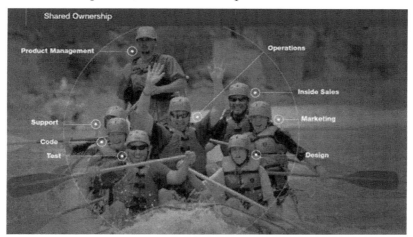

    Figure 4.24: Example of shared ownership (Image Source: https://www.scrumalliance.org)

    We've said that agile is a mindset, not a specific set of practices, and many agile teams end up tailoring their agile methodology to their own circumstances.

126.   Provide a Scrum Checklist sample.

Answer: Let's depict a sample SCRUM checklist:

***Figure 4.25:** Sample Scrum checklist (Image Source: https://www.scrumalliance.org)*

Conclusion

Now that the Scrum master's profession is in such demand, this career ranks 10th on the list of the most promising jobs. A professional Scrum master's salary ranges from $107,280 to $136,748 per annum. Having a certification adds value to an applicant's resume.

There are many interview questions that do not have a right or wrong answer. It all depends on each organization and the applicant's perspective when resolving the situation. So, one should also be prepared for general questions.

Conclusion

Figure 4.26: Conclusion (Image Source: https://www.scrumalliance.org)

In this chapter, we mainly covered:

- Real-life Agile Scrum KANBAN Job interviews questions and answers
- The concept(s) of Agile, Scrum, Kanban
- Applying Agile, Scrum, Kanban in your organization/project(s)
- Numerous tips & tricks to gain new customers by adopting and implementing Agile SCRUM Kanban in organizations/projects/programs and field rules for faster performance & better results
- Field rules for faster performance and better results
- Critical success factors of adopting Agile over the Waterfall model

Parents, students, Scrum masters, product owners, developers, and professionals closely associated with Agile Scrum, Kanban, XP projects can further improve their knowledge of Agile with valuable pragmatic insights. Entry-level professionals and Agile enthusiasts with relevant experience can also acquire in-depth knowledge of the concepts discussed in the Agile methodology tutorial.

In the next chapter, you should be able to go over the:

- Glossary of common Agile Kanban scrum terms

Let's go over some review questions.

Questions

1. **Under which Agile Project phase is "Rework effort" being defined?**
   Select the correct answer(s):
   a. Initiation
   b. Envisioning
   c. Speculate
   d. Explore
   e. Close

2. **You are going to calculate project management metrics "Rework Effort %."**
   Select the correct answer(s):
   Rework Effort % =
   a. (Total Effort expended on Rework across all stages) / (Actual Overall Project Effort) *100
   b. (Total Effort expended on Rework across all stages) * (Actual Overall Project Effort) *100
   c. (Total Effort expended on Rework across all stages) + (Actual Overall Project Effort) *100
   d. (Total Effort expended on Rework across all stages) - (Actual Overall Project Effort) *100
   e. (Total Effort expended on Rework across all stages) ^ (Actual Overall Project Effort) *100

3. **What are true about Rework Effort % (Project Management Metrics)?**
   a. It is "Percentage of Effort expended on Rework activities in the project to overall Effort"
   b. The objective of this metrics is to monitor that effort spent on rework is kept to a minimum
   c. It should be measured at the overall project level
   d. Input is "Total Effort for Rework" and "Total Effort for Project"
   e. It is not metrics

4. **You are going to calculate metrics "Defect Injection Rate (w.r.t Effort)."**
    Select the correct answer(s):

    Defect Injection Rate (w.r.t Effort) =

    a. (Number of In-Process Defects + Number of Customer Reported Defects) / Total Effort

    b. (Number of In-Process Defects + Number of Customer Reported Defects) * Total Effort

    c. (Number of In-Process Defects + Number of Customer Reported Defects) + Total Effort

    d. (Number of In-Process Defects + Number of Customer Reported Defects) - Total Effort

    e. (Number of In-Process Defects - Number of Customer Reported Defects) / Total Effort

5. **You are going to calculate Project Management Metrics "Defect Removal Efficiency."**
    Select the correct answer(s):

    Defect Removal Efficiency =

    a. (Number of In-Process Defects) *100 / (Number of In-Process Defects + Number of Customer Reported Defects)

    b. (Number of In-Process Defects) *100 * (Number of In-Process Defects + Number of Customer Reported Defects)

    c. (Number of In-Process Defects) *100 ^ (Number of In-Process Defects + Number of Customer Reported Defects)

    d. (Number of In-Process Defects) *100 / (Number of In-Process Defects - Number of Customer Reported Defects)

    e. (Number of In-Process Defects) *100 / (Number of In-Process Defects * Number of Customer Reported Defects)

6. **You are going to calculate Project Management Metrics "Defect Rejection Rate."**
    Select the correct answer(s):

    Defect Rejection Rate =

    a. Number of Defects Rejected / Number of Defects Reported

    b. Number of Defects Rejected * Number of Defects Reported

    c. Number of Defects Rejected + Number of Defects Reported

    d. Number of Defects Rejected - Number of Defects Reported

    e. Number of Defects Rejected ^ Number of Defects Reported

7. **You are going to calculate Project Management Metrics "Cost of Poor Quality (COPQ)."**

    Select the correct answer(s):

    Cost of Poor Quality (COPQ) =

    a. Total Rework Effort / Total Effort in Person Hours

    b. Total Rework Effort * Total Effort in Person Hours

    c. Total Rework Effort + Total Effort in Person Hours

    d. Total Rework Effort - Total Effort in Person Hours

    e. Total Rework Effort ^ Total Effort in Person Hours

8. **You are going to calculate Project Management Metrics "Cost of Review Quality (CORQ)."**

    Select the correct answer(s):

    Cost of Review Quality (CORQ) =

    a. Sum of Review and Rework Effort / Total Effort in Person Hours

    b. Sum of Review and Rework Effort * Total Effort in Person Hours

    c. Sum of Review and Rework Effort + Total Effort in Person Hours

    d. Sum of Review and Rework Effort - Total Effort in Person Hours

    e. Sum of Review and Rework Effort ^ Total Effort in Person Hours

9. **We are working in General Motors Agile Project.**

    Total effort for Rework is 10 Person Days (PD), and total effort for Project is 200 PD. Calculate the "Rework Effort %."

    Select the correct answer(s):

    a. 5%

    b. 2%

    c. 4%

    d. 1%

    e. 3%

10. **You are going to calculate Project Management Metrics "Review Effectiveness."**

    Select the correct answer(s):

    Review Effectiveness =

    a. Total Number of Review defects / Total Number of In-Process Defects

    b. Total Number of Review defects * Total Number of In-Process Defects

    c. Total Number of Review defects + Total Number of In-Process Defects *d.*   Total Number of Review defects - Total Number of In-Process Defects

   e.   Total Number of Review defects ^ Total Number of In-Process Defects

Question Number	Answer	Explanation
1	c	**Correct Answer(s):** c. "Rework effort" is being defined under "Speculate" phase. Thus, the other options are incorrect.
2	a	**Correct Answer(s):** a. "Rework Effort %" = (Total Effort expended on Rework across all stages)/ (Actual Overall Project Effort) *100 So, the other options are incorrect.
3	a, b, c, d	**Correct Answer(s):** a, b, c, d. Rework Effort % is Project Management Metrics. So, option e is incorrect and all other options are correct.
4	a	**Correct Answer(s):** a. Defect Injection Rate (w.r.t Effort) = (Number of In-Process Defects + Number of Customer Reported Defects) / Total Effort. Hence, the other options are incorrect.
5	a	**Correct Answer(s):** a. Defect Removal Efficiency = (Number of In-Process Defects) *100 / (Number of In-Process Defects + Number of Customer Reported Defects) So, the other options are incorrect.
6	a	**Correct Answer(s):** a. Defect Rejection Rate = Number of Defects Rejected / Number of Defects Reported. So, the other options are incorrect.
7	a	**Correct Answer(s):** a. Cost of Poor Quality (COPQ) = Total Rework Effort / Total Effort in Person Hours. Thus, the other options are incorrect.

8	a	**Correct Answer(s):** a.
		Cost of Review Quality (CORQ) =
		Sum of Review and Rework Effort / Total Effort in Person Hours.
		Hence, the other options are incorrect.
9	a	**Correct Answer(s):** a.
		Total Effort for Rework = 10 PD
		Total Effort for Project = 200 PD
		Rework Effort % = (10/200) *100 = 5%.
		So, the other options are incorrect.
10	a	**Correct Answer(s):** a.
		Review Effectiveness =
		Total Number of Review defects / Total Number of In-Process Defects.
		Thus, the other options are incorrect.

CHAPTER 5
Glossary

Introduction

In this chapter, we will mainly cover the following topics. After completing this lesson, you will be able to describe/explain/implement:

- Glossary of common Agile Kanban scrum terms
- Understand the concept of Agile Kanban scrum
- Discuss the types of Agility

Glossary of common Kanban terms as it appears in Kanban from the Inside by Mike Burrows. The book helps readers understand the Kanban Method, connect it with familiar models such as Lean, Agile, and Theory of Constraints, and learn how to implement it step-by-step in their organizations. The reader can learn practical techniques to apply the Kanban Method, always considering the context of the particular situation and the people involved in alphabetical order:

In this chapter, you should be able to:

- Understand the glossary of common Agile Kanban scrum terms

Structure

In this chapter, we will discuss:

- Glossary of common Agile Kanban scrum term

Objectives

After studying this unit, you should be able to:

- Understand the concept of Agile Kanban scrum
- Discuss the types of Agility

Happy learning!

Agenda

A structure, plan, or ordered list of items to be discussed in a formal meeting. The objectives are to provide clarity on the topics to be discussed and indicate the expected outcome from the meeting.

Agile

Agile began as an iterative, collaborative, value-driven approach to developing software. It was originally conceived as a framework to help structure work on complex projects with dynamic, unpredictable characteristics.

Since then, it has evolved into a kind of philosophy or world view with a set of well-articulated values and principles that are common between Agile's many varieties.

Based on our research findings and conversations with top executives, we discovered that Agile methodologies can help spur growth and support digital transformation in an era of high customer demand and fast-emerging market trends. The report shows Agile organizations' experience:

- Faster time to market (60%)
- Faster innovation (59%)
- Improved non-financial results such as customer experience and product quality (59%)
- Improved employee morale (57%)

Agility

This is a mindset and style of working characterized by quick response, flexibility, and adaptability.

Agile behaviors

Those behaviors articulate typical working in an agile way (e.g. being collaborative, self-organizing, customer-focused, empowered, trusting not blaming).

Agile plans

Agile plans may show features (or sets of features) in their order and dependencies and are likely to have been created collaboratively by those who will carry out the planned work. Agile plans tend to be informal or low-tech at the delivery-team level, which can be highly effective although they may be no more than to-do lists or backlogs. Product-based planning can still be used at all levels of the project (including product delivery).

Agile SHIFT

New way of working enables teams to work in agile ways and ensures that the whole organization develops enterprise-wide agility. In doing so, it prepares and supports the organization for transformation.

Agile SHIFT coach

This role ensures that new ways of working are understood and used by everyone involved in the creation of value across the organization.

Agile SHIFT practice

An aspect of working in an agile way, it should be addressed continually.

Agile SHIFT principle

The guiding obligations underpin successful organizational transformation through the application of Agile SHIFT.

Agile SHIFT sponsor

They are responsible for communicating the organizational needs and task priority to the Agile SHIFT team. They are also responsible for funding the team's work.

Agile SHIFT workflow

A simple model that demonstrates the Agile SHIFT steps to enable an iterative way of working.

Agility

See enterprise agility.

Benefit

The measurable improvement resulting from an outcome, perceived as an advantage by one or more stakeholders.

Blocker

This is anything that is stopping the progress of the work.

Canvas

Canvases are typically single-document templates that provide an overview of the scope and predicted benefits of a product/service. They are characterized by the qualities of simplicity, repeatability, transparency, and visibility.

Change

This refers to the event or combination of events enabling an organization, function, or practice to become different in some way from what it was before and deliver added value.

Change-authority

A group or person who may be delegated responsibility for the consideration of requests for change or off-specifications. The change authority may be given a change budget and can approve changes within that budget.

Change team

Change teams are responsible for the delivery of change within a specific area, department, or section of an organization. They could be part of a programme or project or a temporary entity. Alternatively, they could be stable, long-lived teams that own change from design through to development and delivery.

Change The Organization (CTO)

The element in the organization charged with identifying, designing, delivering, embedding, and delivering value from change. CTO people are often the originators of change initiatives. Also refer to run the organization.

Close-out

It represents the final iteration in the Agile SHIFT workflow. It ensures that a recognized closure is achieved for a piece of work or a series of iterations.

Co-creation

This is the process enabling an enterprise and its interested parties to work collaboratively and create value for all parties by improving or developing services and products. Stakeholders include CTO, RTO, external suppliers, users, and customers.

Customer

The person, group, or organization benefitted from the value delivered by the work.

Customer story

It represents an informal, natural language description of one or more features of a piece of work. Customer stories are often written from the perspective of an end user or final customer to better understand the requirements.

Daily stand-up

Daily stand-ups are typically held in the same location and at the same time each day. The meetings are often timeboxed to 15 minutes to keep the discussion brisk but relevant. During the stand-up, each team member answers the following three questions:

- What did you do yesterday?
- What will you do today?
- Are there any blockers in your way?

Deliverables

See outputs.

Delta

This is the difference between where the organization wants to be and where it currently is. It could be measured in terms of capability, performance, or the value delivered. The larger the delta, the greater is the vulnerability of the organization to competitors and disruptors.

Digital transformation

It refers to the integration of digital technology into all areas of an organization, fundamentally changing how it operates and delivers value to customers. It also requires a cultural change within the organization to continually challenge the status quo and innovate.

Disruptor

An entity that changes the way in which an industry or sector operates, especially in a new, more effective, and unexpected way. It may create a market where none existed before. It can be caused by, or expressed through, digital capabilities, channels, or assets.

Enterprise agility

The ability of an organization to move and adapt quickly in response to shifting customer and market needs. Agile SHIFT encourages and enables enterprise agility.

Epic

This is a high-level definition of a requirement that has not been sufficiently refined or understood yet. Eventually, an epic will be refined and broken down into several customer stories or requirements.

Gig economy

A labour market characterized by the prevalence of short-term contracts or freelance work and the absence of a centralized workspace.

Increment

An increment is the sum of the product or service delivered up to the start of the current iteration, plus the delivery of the current iteration.

Inefficient market

A market in which there is a significant gap between what customers require and what the existing organizations are offering.

Iteration

An iteration is a timebox, usually of between one and four weeks, during which work takes place. When there is an initiative comprising several iterations, the length of each iteration, in most cases, is kept the same.

Iteration retrospective

A meeting between the Agile SHIFT team and the Agile SHIFT coach at the end of an iteration to analyse the performance of the team during that iteration. It should take place after the iteration review.

Iteration review

An opportunity for stakeholders and the Agile SHIFT team to review what has been achieved in that iteration, including any demonstration of functionality and value enablement.

ITIL

Best-practice guidance for IT service management.

Kaizen

This is a Japanese philosophy that literally means 'good change' but is widely understood to refer to continual improvement. It involves everyone contributing regularly to make many small beneficial changes that build up over time to improve the way a team or organization works.

Kanban

KANBAN has its origins from the different tools that Taaichi Ohno developed at Toyota to operate the production in a systematic framework.

- It is a set of guidelines on how to adapt the existing delivery methodology such that one may, for example, find bottlenecks more accurately and implement change management more easily
- CAPACITY = WORK + WASTE; COST is not in the ACTIVITY, but in FLOW

Kanban board

This is a board that visually displays the work in a task list or iteration. It is usually made up of a series of columns and/or rows where work items move from left to right as they progress through various states in order to be completed.

Lean

An approach that focuses on improving processes by maximizing value through eliminating waste (such as wasted time and wasted effort).

Lean Start-up

This was originally an approach to creating and managing start-up companies that is now applied to any business to help them quickly deliver products to customers.

Managing Successful Programmes (MSP)

Managing Successful Programmes (MSP) helps organizations and individuals manage their projects, programmes, and services consistently and effectively. MSP provides a proven, best-practice approach for designing and running programmes so that organizations can both deliver their strategies and gain measurable benefits from change. It is part of the Global Best Practice suite of publications.

Multimodal

This is the selection of the ways of working appropriate to the task, team, individuals (including customer, stakeholders, leaders, workers), and context.

Optimal value

Agile SHIFT advocates incremental delivery of optimal value (the most favourable value in any given circumstance) to ultimately achieve the best possible value.

Organizational change management

A collection of concepts, approaches, and tools to prepare, support, and lead individuals, teams, and organizations in making organizational change.

Outcomes

The new operational states resulting from using the outputs of an iteration.

Outputs

The deliverables of a planned activity or project.

Parkinson's law

Derives from the observation that 'work expands to fill the time available for its completion' and that a sufficiently large bureaucracy will generate enough internal work to keep itself 'busy' and justify its continued existence without commensurate output.

PMBOK

The Project Management Body of Knowledge (PMBOK) is an internationally recognized standard that includes the fundamental knowledge, skills, tools, and techniques for project management. The PMBOK Guide, published by the Project Management Institute, defines five basic process groups and 10 knowledge areas typical of almost all projects.

Portfolio

A portfolio is the totality of an organization's investment (or segment thereof) in the changes required to achieve its strategic objectives.

PRINCE2 Agile

PRINCE2 Agile describes how to configure and adapt PRINCE2 so that it can be used in the most effective way when combining it with agile behaviours, concepts, frameworks, and techniques.

PRINCE2

PRINCE2 is the world's most widely adopted project management method used by people and organizations from various industries and sectors. It is a flexible method that guides you through the essentials for managing successful projects, regardless of the type or scale. Built upon seven principles, themes, and processes, PRINCE2 can be tailored to meet an organization's specific requirements.

Principle

An Agile SHIFT principle is a rule that can guide an organization in all circumstances, regardless of changes in its goals, strategies, type of work, or management structure.

Product backlog

Product backlog is a list of requirements (called product backlog items). It is managed by the product owner, who orders the product backlog according the value, risks, dependencies, and business intention.

Product owner

The product owner is responsible for maximizing value and return on investment, and they represent the customer and manage the product backlog.

Programme

A temporary, flexible organization structure created to coordinate, direct, and oversee the implementation of a set of related projects and activities in order to deliver outcomes and benefits related to the organization's strategic objectives. A programme is likely to have a life that spans several years.

Programme management

This is the action of carrying out coordinated organization, direction, and implementation of a dossier of projects and transformation activities to achieve outcomes and realize the benefits of strategic importance.

Project

This refers to a temporary organization that is created for the purpose of delivering one or more business products according to an agreed business case.

Project management

The planning, delegating, monitoring, and control of all aspects of the project and the motivation of those involved to achieve the project objectives within the expected performance targets for time, cost, quality, scope, benefits, and risks.

Relative estimating

An abstract estimating technique that encourages teams to consider the 'size' of a task using only other tasks as a point of reference.

Retrospective

See iteration retrospective.

Roadmap

A high-level view of the general direction of the work being undertaken. It will include the expected delivery dates.

Run The Organization (RTO)

The element in the organization charged with conducting the day-to-day work of the organization. RTO people are often the subject of change initiatives. Also refer to change the organization.

Scrum

Scrum is a simple yet incredibly powerful set of principles and practices that help teams deliver products in short cycles, enabling fast feedback, continual improvement, and rapid adaptation to change.

Scrum is the most commonly used Agile framework. The Scrum Guide defines Scrum as "A framework within which people can address complex adaptive problems, while productively and creatively delivering products of the highest possible value." Scrum is a framework, which means you can use techniques from other Agile processes like XP etc. in Scrum projects.

Scrum master

Scrum master ensures that the Scrum framework is used properly. The Scrum master guides and coaches the team and the product owner. The Scrum master is a servant leader role and removes impediments to enable the team to become productive.

Self-organizing team

Non-hierarchical teams that decide, between themselves, how best to deliver work, without specific direction from outside the team. Work is approached collaboratively, with joint commitment to delivering outcomes.

Service management

It refers to a set of specialized organizational capabilities for enabling value for customers in the form of services.

Skillset

This is the particular combination of relevant skills and abilities held by an individual or group.

Sprint

Sprint is the heartbeat of Scrum. All work in Scrum is done during Sprints. Sprint is a time-boxed duration of time, usually 1-4 weeks long. Sprints start with a Sprint planning meeting and end with a Sprint review and retrospective meeting. Teams develop increments of functionality during Sprints.

Sprint planning

Every Sprint starts with a Sprint planning meeting. The team works with the product owner to plan the work for the upcoming Sprint. They collaborate to help the team select items (requirements) from the product backlog for the upcoming Sprint. The Scrum master facilitates the time-boxed meeting.

Sprint review

At the end of the Sprint, the team gets together with the product owner and stakeholders for the Sprint review. They work together to see what was done during the Sprint and update the product backlog for future work. It is a time-boxed meeting, and the Scrum master facilitates this meeting.

Sprint retrospective

This is the last meeting in the Sprint. The team, the product owner, and the Scrum master work together to reflect on the previous Sprint, i.e., what went well during the Sprint, what didn't go so well, and what can they do to improve? Retrospective provides an opportunity for continuous improvement.

Sprint backlog

The Sprint backlog consists of product bcklog items selected for the Sprint and a plan for delivering these items. Usually, it consists of tasks that are the breakdown of product backlog items. The Sprint backlog is the work that the team will do to turn selected product backlog items into a "Done" increment.

Sprint burndown

The effort remaining for tasks plotted across time (days remaining in Sprint) is called the Sprint burndown. It provides a simple and graphical view of the remaining work across the Sprint.

Stakeholder

This is any individual, group, or organization that can affect or be affected by a piece of work (i.e. a programme, project, activity, or risk).

Start-up (in Agile SHIFT workflow)

This is the first step in the Agile SHIFT workflow that assesses the value of the work being proposed.

Start-up (in wider usage)

This is an entrepreneurial venture, generally a newly emerged-business that aims to suffice a marketplace's needs by developing a viable business model around a process, service, product, or platform.

Swarm

The practice of everyone in the team collectively working on a single task until it is complete, before they move on to tackle other tasks.

Task list

This is a simple list of customer user stories and epics that will be the source of any work undertaken.

Tech-centric

This is used for describing activities that would not exist without computer technology. Although the need being fulfilled may have once been fulfilled by a human, at least in part, a new and non-human method for fulfillment has now been found.

Tech-enabled

This is used for describing previously manual activities that are now automated, with efficiency and effectiveness being improved as a result.

Tech-shift

A term used to describe how the influence of technology has shifted the way we live and work.

Tech-supported

This is used for describing manual activities that have benefited from the involvement of computer-based support for the human element.

Timebox

This is a finite period of time within which one or more activities should take place. Most timeboxes describe the maximum period available; if the activity is completed more quickly, the timebox can be closed early. In the case of an iteration timebox, the period is fixed and no early close is permitted, even if the team has completed all promised tasks. Instead, the team will select further tasks to ensure that it is delivering output until the period ends. Examples range from daily stand-ups with 15-minute timeboxes to longer iterations with fixed timeboxes of four weeks.

Toolkit

A collection of templates, charts, diagrams, and other documents designed to assist and guide the delivery team (and other) professionals in agile working.

Transformation

A distinct change in the way an organization conducts all or part of its business.

Transformational leadership

Transformational leadership is a style of leadership where a leader works with their team to identify a needed transformation, creating a vision to guide the change through inspiration and executing the change in tandem with committed members of a group.

Trigger

The reason for commencing any piece of work, a trigger may arise from anywhere inside or outside an organization.

User story

User story is a format to define requirements. It is one of the techniques to define the requirements on the product backlog. A tool used to write a requirement in the form of who, what, and why.

Value

The benefits delivered in proportion to the resources put into acquiring them.

Velocity

The total work the team is capable of completing in a Sprint is called velocity. When the team is planning its first Sprint, it estimates its velocity. For subsequent Sprints, velocity is the amount of work done by the team in the previous Sprint, and this is a guideline for the team to plan its work.

Vision statement

A concise, motivational description of where an organization aspires to be, through a process of strategic transformation, in the mid- to long-term future.

XP

XP (Extreme Programming) is an Agile software development process that focuses on iterations (time-boxed short development cycles) to improve productivity, quality, and responsiveness. Techniques like pair programming, unit testing, and continuous integration stemmed from XP. Several XP techniques are employed by Scrum teams.

Conclusion

In this chapter, we mainly discussed:

- Glossary of common Agile Kanban scrum terms
- The concept of Agile Kanban scrum
- The types of Agility

Parents, students, Scrum masters, product owners, developers, and professionals closely associated with Agile Scrum, Kanban, and XP projects can further improve their knowledge of Agile with valuable pragmatic insights. Entry-level professionals and Agile enthusiasts with relevant experience can also acquire in-depth knowledge of the concepts discussed in the Agile methodology tutorial.

In the next chapter, we will cover:

- Agile Quiz Session

Let's take a look at some review questions.

Questions

1. **In Scrum, the definition of done is created with the input of everyone except the:**
   a. Development team
   b. Product owner
   c. Scrum master
   d. Process owner
   e. Both a and b

2. **Which of the following Agile Manifesto principles reflects the agile focus on team empowerment?**
   a. Working software is the primary measure of progress
   b. Welcome changing requirements, even late in development
   c. Simplicity—the art of maximizing the amount of work not done — is essential

      d.   Build projects around motivated individuals

      e.   Both b and c

3.   **On an agile project, the definition of done is discussed frequently so that:**

      a.   Functionality can be negotiated until the last responsible moment

      b.   All stakeholders have a clear understanding of what completion means

      c.   Team members get to improve their negotiation skills

      d.   Active listening can reveal requirements that haven't been previously discussed

      e.   Both c and d

4.   **The product owner has told the team how much work will need to be completed in the next iteration. In this scenario:**

      a.   The iteration planning process is proceeding smoothly

      b.   The product owner is overstepping their role

      c.   The product owner is taking over the scrum master's responsibilities for planning

      d.   The team should claim more responsibility for planning in their next retrospective

      e.   Both a and d

5.   **The team believes that it will take 15 hours of effort to write the user guide for the new product they are building. What should their estimate be for the task?**

      a.   15 hours

      b.   18 hours, to add a buffer for distractions and availability issues

      c.   12 hours, since teams tend to overestimate how long a task will take

      d.   12 to 18 hours

      e.   13 hours

6.   **Your team committed to delivering 10 story points this iteration, but it looks like you will only complete 8. You should:**

      a.   Extend the iteration

      b.   Add more resources to the team

      c.   Complete 8 points, and put 2 back in the backlog

      d.   Adjust the iteration plan from 10 points down to 8

      e.   Both a and b

7. **The project management office is auditing your agile project and asks to see your iteration plans. They notice that only the next couple of iterations have plans. As a result, they give the project a "red flag" for having incomplete plans. The most responsible thing to do is:**

    a. Explain the agile principles of progressive elaboration and rolling wave planning

    b. Create detailed iteration plans for the remainder of the project

    c. Ignore them, since they clearly have no right to be reviewing your project

    d. Ask the team to create detailed plans for the remaining iterations in the release

    e. Both b and d

8. **You are leading a team with an average velocity of 50 points per iteration. Another team of the same size in your organization is working on a project with similar complexity. The other team's velocity is averaging 75 points per month. Your team should:**

    a. Perform affinity estimating to check their estimates since something is off

    b. Work longer hours

    c. Ignore the difference

    d. Request additional resources to get more work done

    e. Both a and b

9. **Your team is averaging 40 story points per two-week iteration. They have 200 points' worth of functionality left in the user story backlog. How many weeks can we expect it will take until development is completed?**

    a. 2.5

    b. 5

    c. 10

    d. 20

    e. 15

10. **Your lead engineer just came down with the measles in the middle of a sprint. As team coach, what should you do?**

    a. Call his functional manager and request a new lead engineer for your team

    b. Ask the team how much of the planned work can be done

    c. Ask everyone else to work overtime

     d.   Postpone the release date

     e.   Both a and c

11.   **Under which Agile Project phase is "team capability" being accomplished? Select the correct answer(s):**

     a.   Initiation

     b.   Envisioning

     c.   Speculate

     d.   Explore

     e.   Close

12.   **Two team members are having a difference of opinion about how to build the next user story. What should be done?**

     a.   The team coach should assess the level of conflict and intervene appropriately

     b.   The ScrumMaster should decide the issue, since it is becoming an impediment to progress

     c.   The product owner should be consulted

     d.   The team should gather to discuss the issue and come up with a collective solution

     e.   Both a and b

13.   **As the Scrum master, you have been asked to explain to the business what the project team has accomplished during Iteration 0. Which of the following tools would you use for this presentation?**

     a.   Technical debt burnup chart

     b.   Risk burndown graph

     c.   Risk-adjusted backlog

     d.   Average defects per release

     e.   Both a and d

14.   **As the team's agile coach, you measure small amounts of variance in task durations. What should you do?**

     a.   Undertake root cause analysis to eliminate it

     b.   Engage the team in diagnosing the problem

     c.   Diagnose the issue as part of your leadership role

     d.   Accept some variance as inevitable

     e.   Both a and b

15. **As a team member, if you encounter a tricky problem during a development iteration, agile recommends that you:**

    a. Stop what you're doing until you figure out a solution, using your individual expertise and ingenuity

    b. Tell the Scrum master about the problem and let them decide what to do about it, as it's their job to remove impediments to progress

    c. Just keep moving ahead so your velocity isn't disrupted since most problems eventually take care of themselves

    d. Quickly bring the problem

    e. Both a and b

16. **What is the least likely reason why changes found later in the project are more costly to fix?**

    a. More rework might be needed to fix the problem

    b. More stakeholders might be affected by the problem

    c. More code might have to be refactored

    d. More features might have to be supported

    e. Both a and c

17. **We are working in Unilever Agile Scrum project. The product owner is frustrated because the team's estimates are always too low. Each time it turns out that some necessary steps were left out, such as testing or integration, but the variance isn't consistent. How should the product owner address this issue?**

    a. Add a multiplication factor to the estimates based on the worst-case variance from the team's estimate to the actual duration

    b. Visit the team room every day to ensure that they are using the most efficient approach to get the work done

    c. Discuss each estimate with the team to ensure that all the work involved in building the story is included

    d. Agile methods don't require accurate estimate, knowledge work is inherently variable and cannot accurately be estimated

    e. Both a and b

18. **Your team has run into a tricky question about a stakeholder's requirements that is holding up their progress. However, he is travelling and isn't available for an in-person meeting. What should you do?**

    a. Call him on the phone

    b. Send him an email

    c. Wait until he's back in the office to meet face to face

d. Ask another stakeholder what he needs

e. Both b and d

Question Number	Answer	Explanation
1	d	**Correct Answer(s):** d. The whole team, including the development team, product owner, and Scrum master, is responsible for creating the shared definition of done. Since "process owner" is a made-up term, this is the correct choice for someone who would NOT be involved in defining done.
2	d	**Correct Answer(s):** d. Agile Manifesto principle five, "Build projects around motivated individuals" addresses the importance of giving teams the environment and support they need, and trusting them to get the job done. Supporting and trusting the team members means recognizing that they are experts at what they do, and that they can work most effectively if they are empowered to plan and organize their own work.
3	b	**Correct Answer(s):** b. The reason we have frequent discussions about the definition of done is to prevent the mismatches that can occur when different people interpret the descriptions of new functionality in different ways. The definition of done is not intended to be used to negotiate functionality, improve negotiation skills, or surface new requirements (although that may occur). Instead, we have these discussions to ensure that everyone has a common understanding of what completion or success will look like.
4	b	**Correct Answer(s):** b. During iteration planning, the product owner's role is to prioritize the backlog items. The team then decides how many of the top-priority items in the backlog can be completed in the next iteration timebox. So, this product owner is overstepping their role since the amount of work that can be completed in the next iteration is decided by the team, not the product owner or the Scrum master. While it's true that the team isn't doing their own planning based on the information provided in this scenario, it isn't clear that there is a problem on their side that should be addressed in retrospection. The product owner probably just needs to be educated about agile and encouraged to allow the team to do their own planning.

5	a	**Correct Answer(s):** a. Agile teams estimate tasks in ideal time —how long it will take if there are no interruptions or distractions. In this case, they have decided that the effort will take 15 hours, so their estimate should also be 15 hours. If they think the work will take 15 hours, then they wouldn't estimate less than that (and in general, teams tend to underestimate how long a job will take, not overestimate it). Although agile teams rely on estimate ranges to convey the uncertainty of larger estimates to stakeholders, tasks are typically given single-point estimates. That's because those estimates are only for the team, and also, at this point (shortly before the work is done), they should have enough information to agree upon a single-point estimate rather than using a wide range such as 12 to 18 hours.
6	c	**Correct Answer(s):** c. Since iterations are timeboxed, the duration won't be changed. You also wouldn't change the iteration plan or expand the team. Instead, work that isn't completed within the iteration is returned to the backlog. So, the choice of completing 8 points and returning 2 points to the backlog is the correct option.
7	a	**Correct Answer(s):** a. An incomplete set of iteration plans may be a surprise to a PMO that is not familiar with agile methods. When faced with this situation, you should explain the benefits of agile planning and how an agile approach ties into the concepts of progressive elaboration and rolling wave planning. Making up plans too early is a poor use of time on an agile project and could mislead stakeholders. The choice of ignoring the request is incorrect.
8	c	**Correct Answer(s):** c. Velocity is team-specific and unique to a particular team. In other words, a story point for one team probably wouldn't have the same value as a story point for another team. So, it is not appropriate to compare velocities between teams. The best choice would be to ignore the difference.
9	c	**Correct Answer(s):** c. Since this question doesn't indicate any differences in the team's availability or known distractions going forward, we can do a fairly straightforward calculation to get the answer. If we average 40 points per iteration, we should get through a 200-point backlog in 5 iterations (200 / 40 = 5). Each iteration is 2 weeks long, so 5 iterations is equivalent to 10 weeks (5 x 2 = 10). The key to answering this question correctly is noticing that the question is asked for the number of weeks, not the number of iterations.

10	b	**Correct Answer(s):** b. This question tests your grasp of the agile principle of timeboxing. The correct answer is to discuss with the team how much of the planned work they will be able to complete within the timebox. We wouldn't request a new lead engineer, either temporarily or permanently, because swapping people in and out of the team would likely throw the team back to the Storming stage, lowering productivity. The option of asking everyone to work overtime isn't consistent with the agile principle of sustainable development. Although postponing the release date might be necessary in some cases, we aren't given enough information to support the conclusion that it is the best answer.
11	d	**Correct Answer(s):** d. "Team capability" is being accomplished under the Explore phase.
12	d	**Correct Answer(s):** d. On an empowered agile team, it is up to the team members to resolve their technical disputes collectively. The coach, Scrum master, or product owner is unlikely to have the knowledge required to make such decisions.
13	b	**Correct Answer(s):** b. Since Iteration 0 is concerned with establishing tools and environments and proving approaches, a risk burn-down graph would be a good way to show what the team has been working on. While they may not have built any business functionality, hopefully they will have reduced some technical risks and proven some of the key approaches that will be used. The other tools are either made-up terms (technical debt burnup chart) or not relevant to the task at hand (risk-adjusted backlog and average defects per release).
14	d	**Correct Answer(s):** d. The question states that the variance amounts are small. Since some amount of variance is inevitable, we should simply accept it. It would be inappropriate to undertake root cause analysis or take more time to try to diagnose this variation since it is due to common causes.

15	d	**Correct Answer(s):** d. Agile teams rely on collective problem solving rather than individual ingenuity because problems are solved more quickly and effectively when diverse viewpoints are brought to bear, rather than when team members try to push through on their own. And although it is the Scrum master's role to remove impediments to progress, that refers to external roadblocks. When it comes to development issues, in many cases only the team members have the expertise needed to resolve the issue, so those kinds of problems can't be delegated to the Scrum master. Also, one thing we definitely don't want to do is ignore a problem and hope it will go away; that's a sure-fire recipe for technical debt, if not project failure.
16	d	**Correct Answer(s):** d. The first three options are all classic reasons why the cost of change goes up over time. That leaves option D, "more features might have to be supported." Now, this statement could be interpreted as yet another reason why changes would be more costly, but the need to support more features isn't necessarily related to the cost of change. So this is the option least likely to affect the cost of change, and therefore, the correct answer.
17	c	**Correct Answer(s):** c. The best answer here is to work with the team to ensure that all the work involved in building the story is included in their estimates. The other answers aren't consistent with the agile approach. If the team's estimates aren't accurate, they should be using the feedback to learn how to improve the next time. Micromanaging the team is unproductive and conflicts with the agile value of empowering the team. And finally, accurate estimates are essential for agile projects, just like any other project. Although agile estimates start out coarse-grained, they are progressively refined over time to reach a high degree of accuracy.
18	a	**Correct Answer(s):** a. On a fast-moving project, we can't always wait for a face-to-face meeting to address a question. We also don't want to ask someone else to speak for the stakeholder, as it could lead to confusion and miscommunication. So, the remaining options are phone and email. Although email would provide richer communication about a complicated issue. So, the correct answer would be to give him a call.

CHAPTER 6
Quiz Session

Introduction

In this chapter, we will mainly discuss the following topics. After completing this lesson, you will be able to describe/explain/implement:

- Agile quiz session
- Understand the concept of KANBAN
- Apply KANBAN in your organization(s)/project(s)

In this chapter, we will cover:

- KANBAN Quiz
- PMI-ACP and SAFe exam preparation sample questionnaire

Happy learning!

Structure

In this chapter, we will cover the KANBAN Quiz session(s)

Objectives

After studying this unit, you should be able to:

- Understand the concept of KANBAN
- Apply KANBAN in your organization(s)/project(s)

Let's look at some review questions.

Agile Quiz Session
Kanban Exam Sample Questions & Answers

Total Questions: 60   *Total Time: 120 Minutes*

1. **Kanban helps to:**
   a. Become more comfortable to go to Gemba and perform an auditing
   b. Smoothly implement the Agile and Lean management methods in companies
   c. Keep the workplace safe, clean, and organized
   d. None of these

2. **Which of the following is NOT a principle of the Kanban system?**
   a. Limit WIP
   b. Visualize work
   c. Continuity management
   d. Continual improvement

3. **Which two practices are available in making the production process more efficient?**
   a. Production Smoothing and Process Synchronization
   b. Process Synchronization and Load Balancing
   c. Production Smoothing and Load Balancing
   d. Production System and Load Balancing

4. **Which statement is correct about Kanban?**
   a. Kanban is about revolution, not evolution
   b. Kanban is not about revolution; it is about evolution
   c. Kanban is a project management method
   d. None of these

5. **The workflow mapping exercise helps to:**
   a. Encapsulate all politics of the group
   b. Handle and visualize Agile projects

  c. Recognize and correct bottlenecks

  d. None of the above

6. **Production Smoothing is known as:**

  a. A process of monitoring various organizational products' production

  b. A process of breaking various organizational products' production

  c. A process of synchronizing various organizational products' production

  d. A process of streamlining various organizational products' production

7. **Is "visualizing the work" in a Kanban system a crucial step?**

  a. True

  b. False

8. **According to the step 2 exercise, the team member places their sticky notes on the whiteboard that corresponds to the:**

  a. Current status of the production

  b. Current status of the work item

  c. Current status of the bottlenecks

  d. All of the above

9. **How do you calculate the Required Quantity per day in a Kanban system?**

  a. Required Quantity per day = Required Quantity per month / Number of days of operation

  b. Required Quantity per day = Number of days of operation / Required Quantity per month

  c. Required Quantity per day = Number of days of operation / Required Quantity per year

  d. Required Quantity per day = Number of weeks of operation / Required Quantity per month

10. **According to the step 2 activity (Sample Board and Card Example), "Ticket ID #42" is a:**

  a. Activity name

  b. Name of the card

  c. Unique identifier based on team standards

  d. None of the above

11. **The best method that could be used to observe the workflow is a:**

    a. Regular interview

    b. Regular meeting

    c. Regular report

    d. All of the above

12. **Which of the following is the correct formula for calculating takt time?**

    a. Takt time = Available daily production time / Required daily quantity of input

    b. Takt time = Available daily production cost / Required daily quantity of output

    c. Takt time = Available daily production cost / Required daily quantity of resources

    d. Takt time = Available daily production time / Required daily quantity of output

13. **"Daily stand-ups" received their name because teams meet while standing, rather than sitting. Why is standing preferred?**

    a. Standing encourages brevity and staying on task

    b. Standing improves concentration

    c. Standing enhances mind alertness

    d. None of these

14. **In which direction does the leader 'walk the board' in the step 3 exercise?**

    a. From left to right

    b. Randomly

    c. From right to left

    d. None of these

15. **On what basis is the takt time measured?**

    a. Employees working on a production line

    b. Units required per day

    c. Employees who don't work on a production line

    d. Units required per annum

16. **The Kanban retrospective is key to:**

    a. Finding improvement opportunities

    b. Finding problems in the system

    c.   Tracking multiple projects on one board

    d.   None of the above

17. **Which feature of a Kanban system makes it different from a usual to-do list?**

    a.   Workflow

    b.   Limiting the WIP

    c.   Motivation

    d.   None of these

18. **Define Load Balancing.**

    a.   The amount of resources that an organization needs

    b.   The amount of time that an organization needs to do work

    c.   The amount of work that an organization is required to complete

    d.   The amount of work that an employee is required to do

19. **Which of the following terms helps reduce the size of the largest queues?**

    a.   Measure the lead time

    b.   Target process

    c.   Visual metrics

    d.   Limit the WIP

20. **Which of the following is NOT considered in the weekly retrospective?**

    a.   Throughput

    b.   Shortened time cycle

    c.   Total blocked days

    d.   Lead time for every card

21. **There are _____ types of Kanban Systems:**

    a.   3

    b.   4

    c.   5

    d.   6

22. **Throughput is the:**

    a.   Number of work items completed per time period

    b.   Number of processes completed per hour

c. Number of processes completed per day

d. None of these

23. **What are the two types of Kanban Cards?**

   a. Process Kanban and Withdrawal Kanban

   b. Production Kanban and Signal Kanban

   c. Production Kanban and Withdrawal Kanban

   d. Signal Kanban and Withdrawal Kanban

24. **The _____ processes of the Toyota system are connected with invisible conveyor lines.**

   a. Internal and external

   b. Downstream and single-stage

   c. Project management

   d. None of these

25. **Withdrawal Kanban is used to:**

   a. Push items from the previous operation

   b. Pull an item from the previous operation

   c. Define an item in the previous operation

   d. Examine the items in the previous operation

26. **Single Kanban uses:**

   a. Production Kanban to block material handling based on the part type

   b. Procurement Kanban to unblock material handling based on the part type

   c. Production Kanban to unblock material handling based on the part type

   d. KAMISHIBAI Boards to block material handling based on the part type

27. **Which of the following is NOT an experimental method in Kanban?**

   a. Hypothesis

   b. Assumptions

   c. Experiment Operation

   d. Experiment Reports

28. **Which conditions are necessary for the appropriate functioning of the Single Kanban System?**

    a. Small buffer space and fast turnover of work in progress

    b. Synchronization between the speed of material handling and production rate

    c. Kanban's fast turnover

    d. All of the above

29. **The basic plan for experiment design is provided by:**

    a. Assumptions

    b. Experiment Design

    c. Experiment Reports

    d. Hypothesis

30. **The Dual Kanban System is suitable for _____ who are not ready to accept stringent control rules for buffer inventory.**

    a. Manufacturers

    b. Software developers

    c. Vendors

    d. None of these

31. **_____ are used to gain understanding as we shift from major stages of development.**

    a. Assumptions

    b. Hypotheses

    c. Experiment Design

    d. Experiment Reports

32. **Which of the following is NOT a characteristic of a Semi-Dual Kanban System?**

    a. Large distance between two stages

    b. Slow turnover of KANBANs

    c. External buffer to the production system

    d. Slow turnover of work in progress

33. **Which of the following is NOT an element of experimental methods?**

    a. Falsifiable hypothesis

    b. Background

    c.   Production Kanban

    d.   Experiment methods

34. **Which of the following Kanban operations is NOT performed in the receiving area?**

    a.   Receiving from storage

    b.   Receiving from the preceding stage in the same facility

    c.   Receiving from a vendor

    d.   None of the above

35. **Surveys, A/B tests, solution interviews, and problem interviews are methods of _____:**

    a.   Experiment methods

    b.   Background

    c.   Experiment results

    d.   Variables and Measures

36. **The number of KANBANs can be calculated based on the _____:**

    a.   Number of work items

    b.   Value of inventory

    c.   Number of prototypes

    d.   None of the above

37. **Which Kanban principle is used in A/B testing?**

    a.   Limit Work in Process

    b.   Focus on Flow

    c.   Continuous improvement

    d.   Visualize work

37. **Choose the missing statement in the formula from the following options:**

=

Number of Kanban

(Maximum daily production quantity) * (production waiting time + production processing time + ? + safety factor)

Standard number of parts (SPN)

    a.   Withdraw lead time

    b.   Withdraw processing time

c. Daily lead time

d. Required daily quantity

38. **The major components of a Kanban Board in the context of cards include:**

a. Name the map

b. Description text

c. Categorizing maps

d. All of the above

40. **_____ is the interval between receiving production command and completing the lot:**

a. Production processing time

b. Production processing cost

c. Production waiting time

d. None of the above

41. **Kanban Cards are _____ in nature:**

a. Hierarchical

b. Non-hierarchical

c. Consistent

d. Non-consistent

42. **The safety factor is based on _____ :**

a. Cost unit

b. Time unit

c. Per unit

d. Risk unit

43. **The predictions of experimental methods are described in _____ :**

a. Experimental results

b. Variables and Measures

c. Background

d. Falsifiable hypothesis

44. **Which of the following is necessary for Kanban systems to work properly?**

a. Periods of high demand mixed with periods of low demand

b. Smooth and consistent push of material

    c. Smooth and consistent pull of material

    d. Project management tools mixed with low demand

45. **Kanban boards provide us with the functionality to limit_____ and make ongoing work visible:**

    a. Work in progress (WIP)

    b. Work Breakdown Structure (WBS)

    c. Use of resources

    d. None of above

46. **Insertion maintenance takes place when the number of Kanbans utilized in a current planning period is _____ the number of Kanbans utilized in the previous period.**

    a. < (Less than)

    b. > (Greater than)

    c. ≤ (Less than or equal to)

    d. ≥ (Greater than or equal to)

47. **_____ type of Kanban describes the number of operations required to produce an item:**

    a. Withdrawal Kanban

    b. Emergency Kanban

    c. Supplier Kanban

    d. Production Kanban

48. **_____ takes place when the number of KANBANs utilized in the ongoing planning period is less than number of KANBANs utilized in the previous period:**

    a. Insertion maintenance action

    b. Removal maintenance action

    c. Insertion maintenance system

    d. Emergency maintenance system

49. **How many principles does Kanban have?**

    a. 2

    b. 3

    c. 4

    d. 5

50. **From the following options, select the missing statement in the "create a continuous loop of material and signals" diagram:**

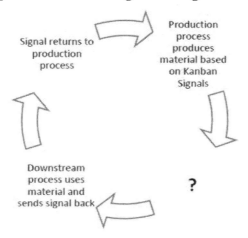

Figure 6.1: Material and signals diagram

   a. Materials and Kanban signal awaits use in downstream processes

   b. Materials and Kanban signal awaits use in upstream processes

   c. KAMISHIBAI and Kanban signal awaits in downstream processes

   d. KAMISHIBAI and Kanban signal awaits in upstream processes

51. **What does Takt Time represent?**

   a. The rate of customer satisfaction

   b. The time to produce a product

   c. The rate of customer demand

   d. Cost required for a particular time period

52. **Which of the following things should be included in the rules of Kanban?**

   a. Any scheduling rules of thumb

   b. The meaning of the scheduling signals and how to interpret them

   c. The part numbers covered by the Kanban

   d. All of the above

53. **Load Balancing is used to maintain a balance between:**

   a. Load and work

   b. Capacity and load

   c. Load and time

   d. Load and volume

54. The _____ should help the production operators make consistent production scheduling decision based on the stated priorities:

    a. Decision Rules

    b. Service Orientation Rules

    c. Project Progression

    d. None of the above

55. Impractical work methods and variations mostly produce materials that are defected.

    a. True

    b. False

56. The _____ visually instructs the working of Kanban:

    a. Visual management plan

    b. Visual development plan

    c. Visual performance system

    d. Visual development system

57. An _____ process never sends bad parts to downstream process:

    a. Upwards

    b. External

    c. Upstream

    d. None of the above

58. Which of the following tips does NOT make a useful impact in making the Visual Aid colourful and easy to read?

    a. Avoid yellow: typically related to safety

    b. Avoid large print for hanging signs and wall signs

    c. Avoid excessive words on signs: people do not read signs, they glance at them

    d. None of the above

59. Kanban Systems are an effective way to fine-tune your:

    a. Production levels

    b. Manufacture levels

    c. Design levels

    d. Marketing levels

60. **Is this statement true or false? Takt time is calculated by comparing volume with working hours.**

    a. True

    b. False

Answer Key

1	*b*	31	*b*
2	*c*	32	*c*
3	*c*	33	*c*
4	*b*	34	*d*
5	*a*	35	*a*
6	*c*	36	*b*
7	*a*	37	*d*
8	*b*	38	*a*
9	*a*	39	*d*
10	*c*	40	*a*
11	*b*	41	*a*
12	*d*	42	*b*
13	*a*	43	*b*
14	*c*	44	*c*
15	*b*	45	*a*
16	*a*	46	*b*
17	*b*	47	*d*
18	*c*	48	*b*
19	*d*	49	*c*
20	*b*	50	*a*
21	*d*	51	*c*
22	*a*	52	*d*
23	*c*	53	*b*
24	*a*	54	*a*
25	*b*	55	*a*
26	*a*	56	*a*
27	*c*	57	*c*

28	*d*	58	*b*
29	*c*	59	*a*
30	*a*	60	*a*

Conclusion

In this chapter, we mainly discussed:

- Agile quiz session
- The concept of KANBAN
- Applying KANBAN in your organization(s)/project(s)

The parents, students, scrum masters, product owners, developers, and professionals closely associated with Agile Scrum, Kanban, and XP projects can further improve their knowledge of Agile with valuable pragmatic insights. Entry-level professionals and Agile enthusiasts with relevant experience can also acquire in-depth knowledge of the concepts discussed in the Agile methodology tutorial.

Happy learning!

Printed in Germany
by Amazon Distribution
GmbH, Leipzig